BUSINESS, THE UNIVERSE & EVERYTHING

STUART CRAINER AND DES DEARLOVE

BUSINESS, THE UNIVERSE & EVERYTHING

CONVERSATIONS WITH THE WORLD'S GREATEST MANAGEMENT THINKERS

CAPSTONE

Copyright © Suntop Media, 2003

The right of Suntop Media to be identified as the author of this book has been asserted in accordance with the Copyright, Designs and Patents Act 1988

First published 2003 by

Capstone Publishing Limited (A Wiley Company)
The Atrium
Southern Gate
Chichester
West Sussex PO19 8SQ
http://www.wileyeurope.com

All Rights Reserved. Except for the quotation of small passages for the purposes of criticism and review, no part of this publication may be reproduced, stored in a retrieval system or transmitted in any form or by any means, electronic, mechanical, photocopying, recording, scanning or otherwise, except under the terms of the Copyright, Designs and Patents Act 1988 or under the terms of a licence issued by the Copyright Licensing Agency Ltd, 90 Tottenham Court Road, London W1T 4LP, UK, without the permission in writing of the Publisher. Requests to the Publisher should be addressed to the Permissions Department, John Wiley & Sons Ltd, The Atrium, Southern Gate, Chichester, West Sussex PO19 8SQ, England, or emailed to permreq@wiley.co.uk, or faxed to (+44) 1243 770571.

CIP catalogue records for this book are available from the British Library and the US Library of Congress

ISBN 1-84112-562-8

Typeset in 10.5/13 pt Minion
by Sparks Computer Solutions Ltd
http://www.sparks.co.uk
Printed and bound by
TJ International Ltd, Padstow, Cornwall

Substantial discounts on bulk quantities of Capstone Books are available to corporations, professional associations and other organizations. For details telephone John Wiley & Sons on (+44-1243-770441), fax (+44-1243-770571) or e-mail CorporateDevelopment@wiley.co.uk

CONTENTS

Preface vii
Acknowledgements ix
About the Authors xi

Section 1: Leading the Way 1

Warren Bennis: Geeks, geezers and beyond 3
Rosabeth Moss Kanter: Teaching cowboys Confucius 7
Manfred Kets de Vries: The dark side of leadership 12
John Kotter: In the field 18
Daniel Goleman: Maxed emotions 23

Section 2: Selling the Future 35

Peter Schwartz: Thinking the unthinkable 37
Watts Wacker: Fringe benefits 42
John Patrick: The attitude thing 46
Charles Handy: Reflections of a reluctant capitalist 52
Philip Kotler: Marketing in the digital age 64

Section 3: People Power 69

Derrick Bell: The ardent protestor 71
Jonas Ridderstråle: Emotional capital 79
Leif Edvinsson: The context's the thing 83
Tony Buzan: Brain power 87
Marshall Goldsmith: Coaching for results 93
Kjell Nordström: Tribal gathering 98
Tom Stewart: Intellectual capitalist 102

Section 4: Strategic Wisdom — 107

    Gary Hamel: The radical fringe — 109
    Costas Markides: Escaping the jungle — 114
    James Champy: What re-engineering did next — 121
    W Chan Kim and Renée Mauborgne: Strategic moves — 126
    Henry Mintzberg: Searching for balance — 132
    Sumantra Ghoshal: The rise of the volunteer investor — 137

    Index — 143

PREFACE

Business thinking and best practice is in a constant state of flux. In the business world, ideas change things and ideas are constantly themselves being changed. As you read, a factory in China could be contemplating re-engineering, a start-up in Stockholm may be coming to terms with one-to-one marketing and a Greek conglomerate examining the merits of intellectual capital.

Ideas are constantly being put to work. If you're sceptical, look at the big idea of the 1990s: re-engineering. The idea was popularized by a book – *Re-engineering the Corporation* by James Champy and Michael Hammer. It was hailed as a revolution. The book sold in hundreds of thousands. People everywhere began re-engineering. At one time, most of the world's leading companies were re-engineering. In the business world, ideas aren't decorative; they are acted upon.

Of course, making things happen is more difficult than any of the bright ideas ever suggest. The practical usefulness of many of the ideas is questionable. If you read Nick Hornby and buy an Arsenal soccer shirt you do not become Thierry Henry. Read Charles Handy and you do not find yourself automatically transplanted into a shamrock organization in possession of a portfolio career.

While there may be nothing so practical as a neat theory, you still have to find the right theory. This is a book awash with bright business ideas from some of world's leading business thinkers. It will not turn a bad business into a good business. Nor will it turn a bad businessman into an entrepreneurial genius. Life – and business life – isn't like that.

However, what this collection of interviews offers is a smorgasbord of business ideas. Pick and choose. Some you will find risible. Others will strike a chord. Others still you may remember and act on. In the final analysis, ideas are nothing without application.

Stuart Crainer and Des Dearlove
May 2003

ACKNOWLEDGEMENTS

We would first like to thank all of the people interviewed for this collection. Their time and insights are greatly and continually appreciated.

All of the interviews in the book were conducted in 2002 and 2003. Inevitably, conversations came around to the events dominating the headlines. We have left such topical comments and remarks in the interview texts. They come, therefore, with the caveat that they were spoken without the benefit of hindsight.

Many of these interviews were first published in newspapers and magazines around the world through our syndication series. This is expertly managed by James Nelson of Knowledge Curve.

We would also like to thank our colleagues at Suntop Media – Steve Coomber for his invaluable help and Georgina Peters for being there. Plus a big thank you to Rick Comber for his wonderful caricatures.

ABOUT THE AUTHORS

Stuart Crainer and Des Dearlove are the founders of Suntop Media (www.suntopmedia.com). They both contribute a column to *The Times*. They are contributing editors to *Strategy+Business* and *Chief Executive*.

Stuart and Des are the authors of a number of books. These include *The Financial Times Handbook of Management*, *Gravy Training* and *Generation Entrepreneur*. Their books have been translated into 20 languages.

At Suntop Media, Stuart and Des have launched the first ever ranking of management gurus, the Thinkers 50 (www.thinkers50.com), and developed their highly successful Business Writing Masterclasses.

Section 1
LEADING THE WAY

People have been debating what makes great leaders for centuries – certainly as far back as Homer and the Ancient Greeks. Theories abound. *Great Man* theories, popular in the nineteenth and early twentieth centuries, were based on the notion of the born leader with innate talents that could not be taught. *Trait Theory*, an alternative approach and still in vogue, identifies the key traits of effective leaders. *Behaviourist Theory* views leadership in terms of what leaders do rather than their characteristics, identifying the different roles they fulfil. *Situational Theory* sees leadership as specific to the situation rather than the personality of the leader.

Today, leadership is a hardy perennial of business book publishing. More than 2000 books on leadership are published every year. But, a small rainforest and an ocean of ink later, we are still searching for definitive answers.

Certainly traditional leadership models are buckling under the weight of expectation. The modern leader has multiple roles and constituencies. The job is increasingly fragmented. There is little time to do everything well and so he or she faces a continuing series of trade-offs of time, energy and focus. Increasingly, too, these demands create seemingly contradictory pressures. At present many leaders face an agonizing dilemma. They are under pressure to cut costs. Yet, at the same time, they know that the dot-com bust notwithstanding, the Internet and other digital technologies offer enormous opportunities. Leaders are caught between the proverbial rock and a hard place. They must create value through performance delivered today, while at the same time sowing the seeds of innovation for tomorrow.

This too is not an either/or situation. Shareholders now expect them to deliver on both fronts simultaneously – and that's a tall order. Connecting the dots has never been more important, or more difficult. Leaders themselves admit that the role is becoming more challenging. They cite pressure from financial institutions to meet performance expectations, increasing complexity and competitiveness of business as a result of globalization, restructuring and managing change, increasingly demanding customers, difficulties in finding good people, and technological change, particularly the use of information technology. The fact is that the job of leaders has never been so hard; or shareholders so unforgiving.

A rising failure rate among CEOs suggests it is time to reinvent leadership for the challenges of the twenty-first century. For the moment, heroic leadership is out of favour with the theorists. (Though it is probably unrealistic to think that the days of heroic leadership are over. After all, Winston Churchill was recently voted the greatest Briton of all time and Abraham Lincoln is still an icon in the US.) Theorists argue that the idea that one person is responsible for the success of an entire nation or a multinational company is absurd.

New models of leadership are emerging. A more holistic view of leadership is being adopted. Take transformational leadership for example, one idea that has steadily gained ground. It connects with other fashionable leadership ideas such as inspirational leadership, visionary leadership and 'emotional intelligence'. It embraces the role of followers and acknowledges the need for all in an organization to embrace leadership. Issues such as spirituality, and certainly ethics, are now more closely identified with business leadership. Perhaps because of this, leadership is increasingly seen in the context of values. The actions of the leader are expected to be driven by clearly articulated values rather than by short-term business imperatives.

Whether the new leadership styles will stand the test of time remains to be seen. On one hand, the new leader is expected to be modest, unpretentious, engaging, flexible, diplomatic, ethical, even humble. Yet that same person is expected to deal confidently with a rapacious media, boldly carry off audacious deals, and fearlessly take on competitors. Truly great leaders, it seems, require a perplexing combination of apparently incompatible characteristics.

WARREN BENNIS: GEEKS, GEEZERS AND BEYOND

Warren Bennis has done more to debunk the heroic leadership myth than just about any other business thinker. Leaders, he argues, are made not born. Usually ordinary – or apparently ordinary – people rather than charismatic or talismanic stereotypes; the heroic view of the leader, he believes, is now outdated and inappropriate. 'The new leader is one who commits people to action, who converts followers into leaders, and who can convert leaders into agents of change', says Bennis.

From his base at the University of Southern California in Los Angeles, where he is founder of the University's Leadership Institute, Bennis has produced a steady stream of books, including the bestselling Leaders *and, most recently,* Geeks and Geezers *which compares leaders under the age of 35 ('geeks') with those over 70 ('geezers').*

Now in his late 70s, Bennis' intellectual energy and output remain formidable. He talked in his new office in Harvard Business School where he is spending time as an advisor on leadership.

What motivated you to compare young and old leaders?

I want to understand human development. I think that's the new challenge. In the future we will see chairs in cognitive psychology and human development established in schools of business. Human development will be an integral part of leadership curricula. That's what I would have gone into if I was deciding now. There are two basic things that I'm really excited about and want to understand.

The first is that when I go out and talk to my students, who are 20-year-olds, and young executives, I'm not sure I really understand how they see the world. These people are visual, digital, and virtual. I want to understand what their aspirations are; how they perceive the world; how they define success; what their career goals are. Basically, what provides the meaning in their lives.

The second group, the 70-plus leaders, are all people who manage to keep their minds open and continuously reinvent themselves. I want to know why these people keep growing and why other people get stuck. I've seen people in their 40s who are on a treadmill to oblivion. But these older leaders are still hungry for growth. Why?

Aren't the older leaders – the geezers – inevitably more interesting than the geeks?

I am one of them so I would hate to sound biased or judgemental but they have lived longer and gone through an awful lot. I think what the geeks haven't experienced are the crucibles like World War II and the Depression. They have had formative years of almost uninterrupted prosperity, growth and success. They are often children of affluence. So 9/11 was the first collective shock to the world view they grew up with. It was a jolt to them.

You talk of the geeks being smothered in possibilities.

The world's their oyster and they can choose what they do. I think it does create anxiety. They have so many options and possibilities.

You argue that crucibles are important in people's development. But can you create your own crucible?

That's the big question. I think they are created all the time. Having to fire people, being fired, being shipped to an office you don't like, thinking that you have been demoted when maybe you haven't. My concern is how we use such everyday crucibles which we're not sometimes conscious of. We all experience crucibles but what do we do at the back end of them? Do we learn from them? Do we extract wisdom from them? It isn't a question of how we create them; they happen and happen almost all the time. But do we think of them as a dream so that when we wake up and brush our teeth it vaporizes or do we think about the dream and learn from that?

But you can't be held responsible for the era in which you live.

President Clinton was always slightly envious that he didn't have a war to deal with, to prove himself. Teddy Roosevelt was the same, though he had a few minor skirmishes.

You could look at this generation of geeks and say that their formative period ended at 9/11 but it started in 1989 when the Berlin Wall fell, the Cold War ended, and then came the introduction of the World Wide Web. So it's not a generational thing, it is a shorter period.

So leaders have to seek out uncertainty?

In the final analysis, you can't create Mandela's Robyn Island or John McCain's experiences as a prisoner of war in Vietnam. They are extreme.

Your experiences in World War II were obviously a crucible for you, but did you emerge from that thinking of yourself as a leader?

What I learned was discipline and a sense of self-mastery. It shaped me so much and pulled from me things I may never have experienced. I was very shy and felt that I was a boring human being, and then in the course of being in the army I felt that I was more interesting to myself. It was a coming of age.

Do you detect that same level of self-awareness in the young business leaders you talked to?

I think they feel that they have more license to talk about themselves and their inner feelings. Unlike some of the geezers who would never dream about talking about their relationships with their family and so on. There is a real restraint among the geezers, a kind of reserve, while the younger generation are more free with their feelings, aspirations and things like that.

What about the way we develop leaders. A lot of people appear to go on MBA programmes without a bedrock of self-awareness.

You've got to realize that most business school faculty have not actually run anything. They have not done the heavy lifting of actually leading. I am glad now that business schools are taking people who have worked for three or five years. In many instances they have more experience than the faculty.

I am in favour of a national service system. It is badly needed. The youth are all dressed up but have no place to go. This would not be military service – though I wouldn't exclude the military – so they could get experience before going to law school or business school.

There is a required course on ethics at Harvard Business School but not at most business schools. It's a very difficult topic but we need to think about the purpose of education. We have to ask the question at business schools, is there something more important than money? Do corporations exist for something more than money and the bottom line? Of course they do, but we have to explain it better.

Was there a difference between the geeks and the geezers in terms of their attitudes to money?

The geezers were brought up in Maslowian survival mode. Often they grew up in some poverty with limited financial aspirations. They thought that earning $10,000 a year would be enough. Compare that to the geeks, some of whom made a lot of money when they were young. They are operating out of a different context. If they were broke they would be more concerned with making a living than making history.

How can you bridge the gap between the geeks and the geezers?

We must. After all, we are going to have to get used to a lot more geezers like me walking around. I think the geezers may have a more difficult time with changes underway – such as technology. You start to think about mortality in your 60s and there is a certain envy towards youth. In your 60s you are no longer promising.

The dialogue between generations is important. It is the people who are in the middle group between the geeks and the geezers, who are comfortable with the technology but a little wiser and older, who have to be the articulating point. They have the responsibility I think to be the translators, the people who will help each group.

A number of companies, including General Electric, have reverse mentoring where young people mentor older people to acquaint them with the e-world. There is a lot of ageism which I probably wouldn't be sensitive to except for the fact I am in my 70s. These will be profound issues for society in general.

How do you rate President Bush's performance as a leader?

I would give President Bush a good mark for being a manager but a low mark for being a leader because he hasn't called on the nation to do much more than shop a little bit more.

ROSABETH MOSS KANTER: TEACHING COWBOYS CONFUCIUS

The Harvard Business School professor Rosabeth Moss Kanter is one of the 100 most important women in America according to one magazine and among the world's 50 most powerful women according to another. There is no doubt that Professor Kanter is intellectually formidable. Her career includes spells at Yale and Harvard Law School. She edited the Harvard Business Review, helped found the consulting firm Goodmeasure, advises the CEOs of major multinationals and is an active Democrat – though her credentials are such that she recently participated in President Bush's gathering of American business minds in Waco, Texas in 2002.

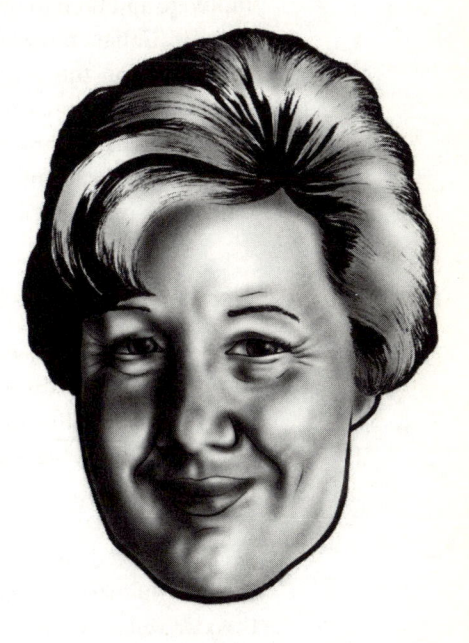

Professor Kanter's work – which includes the bestsellers Change Masters, When Giants Learn to Dance, World Class and Evolve! – combines academic rigour with a degree of idealism not usually found in the bottom-line fixated world of management thinking. Her world view is not confined to the boardroom. Her thesis examined nineteenth century Utopian communities. Rather than leaving her youthful idealism behind, Professor Kanter now brings it to bear on the big business issues. She is a champion of social entrepreneurship as well as a thought leader in change management and globalization.

Most recently, Professor Kanter's ideas have been developed into a Change Toolkit, a Web-based tool that helps people diagnose issues, define projects, and lead change. She explains how it works and her latest thinking on change, leadership and globalization.

Not many leading business thinkers have embraced new technology with your enthusiasm. What's the aim of your Change Toolkit?

I want to create Web-based versions of my work to empower people to make change more effective. I want to give these skills to everyone so that change management – essential to leadership – becomes more widely understood and practiced.

The content consists of 150 interlinked 'tools' – explanations and descriptions, action guides, frameworks, diagnostic tests, etc. – based on my work. It is about putting my theories into action. I believe this is a way to empower people – by giving them the tools to take initiative, to lead and gain confidence in their ability to innovate and then to develop still more leaders. Shared tools shape organizational culture: a common understanding and vocabulary, workspace on the Web to compare notes, to compare scores on diagnostic instruments, and to exchange useful information. The net enables us to translate material from books and workbooks into live, interactive, exciting, dynamic action tools embedded in the daily work of people and organizations.

Do you still regard technology as a force for good?

Yes, I have enormous hopes. Already, there have been tremendous improvements in education and many businesses are more efficient internally. In healthcare, physicians and providers can be empowered through having less paperwork, the ability to get information faster and so on.

The potential of the technology remains great but we're in a period where companies aren't spending money and we're still in the era's infancy. We lived through a period of peace and prosperity then we've had some crises and challenges to some of the assumptions of Western capitalism. Now there's a cooling-off period, but new technology is fundamental and will make a difference.

With an abundance of crises and challenges, do we have unrealistic expectations of our corporate leaders?

Yes, we do if the expectation is that a single leader can do it all. But it is also interesting how much a single leader can set in motion. In turnarounds it is striking how much fresh leadership can accomplish by unlocking talent and potential, which was already there in the organization but was stifled by rules, regulations and bureaucracy.

I wish there were more corporate leaders stepping forward to address the root causes of accounting problems, not simply responding to the rules requiring honest numbers, but talking about the responsibilities businesses have. True leadership means acting before a crisis gets out of hand and not simply being defensive.

Why don't they?

Unsustainable expectations for speedy and continuing growth, for quarterly earnings increases put pressure on companies to get there by all means. Leadership also involves setting realistic performance expectations.

So we need to rethink our understanding of leadership?

Most attempts to understand leadership – in an era in which everyone says we need more leaders, we need better leadership, and the problem is a lack of leadership – deal with individual character, drive, experiences and personality characteristics, or they deal with actions – what do leaders do, how to you create a vision, mobilize a team and so forth.

But if there's character and actions, there are also circumstances. I began to think of this at greater length after September 11, 2001, when New York City Mayor Rudy Giuliani became a hero. That was a very good example of rising to the occasion, of someone who, whatever his character, whatever actions he engaged in before, the circumstances made it possible for him to exhibit a level of leadership which was thought of as exemplary.

But you can't exercise control over circumstances.

You are not always born at the historical moment when you get to create a new country. You're not always living in a time when you can show that your actions made a real difference. Leadership is a combination of being born in the right place, being handed the opportunity, the character of the person, and the support systems.

Is the western heroic view of leadership still appropriate?

If we think of the western notion of leadership as cowboy leadership, the tough heroic stuff, it is no longer very appropriate. My view of leadership is probably more Confucian than cowboy.

The best leaders have somewhat universal characteristics. Leaders are more effective when they are able to create coalitions, develop and use a support system, encourage, listen and develop other people. Those sorts of attributes tend to transcend cultures.

During a lecture tour to South Africa in March 2002, I thought about Nelson Mandela's achievements. He is someone of enormous character but I was struck by the support system surrounding him.

In terms of people?

Yes, in terms of people, in terms of a movement. Nelson Mandela comes from a communal tradition and he is very tough but also very consensus oriented.

His ability to exercise leadership came about because his followers paved the way, and he in turn empowered them. I have always been interested in empowerment – what frees people or encourages them to exercise whatever their natural abilities might be?

How can and should organizations respond to the challenge of rising expectations?

First, they must innovate, improvise quickly. This is a continuing issue. Second, they must work effectively with external partner networks. Third, they must be able to build a sense of community throughout the entire enterprise. Fourth, they must invest in people, not just financially but in the quality of the job and their ability to exercise leadership. Finally, there is corporate citizenship, engaging in activities which are seen as improving the state of the world the company lives in; not simply obeying laws but improving the state of the world.

The final ingredient is essential for employee loyalty and the nature of the brand. Consumers increasingly ask who is this company, what does it stand for, so that's an important piece of the strategic agenda. Corporate citizenship is a means by which a company becomes embedded in a local community, moves from being one of 'them' to become one of 'us'. Companies which have become part of the fabric of the local community are viewed very positively. People are very aware what companies are or are not doing for their community and country.

There's a lot of data that shows that countries which engage in trade by and large have had incomes rise even for people at the bottom. It's just that the gaps are so wide everywhere. My current research suggests that multinationals play a positive role in developing countries by raising certain employment standards when they are actually producing in the countries to sell in those markets; then they have a stake in social and economic development.

Are you optimistic?

I always have a degree of optimism though I think we're in a rough period in which things could get worse before they get better. Right now we have the threat of terrorism, military action and tremendous tension; this has a dampening effect on countries and businesses which have no direct involvement. It creates fear, reduces investment, increases costs and slows down the movement of goods and people.

Then we have the disclosure of corporate ethical lapses and mistakes, which creates crisis. A lot of people have lost a lot of money. Trust in institutions is low. If people don't have trust in the honesty and ethics of leaders that's a problem. In addition, there is the weakness of the economy.

This comes to one of my ultimate definitions of leadership – examining root causes and system issues and not just superficial tinkering. Trying to patch over a bad situation with a little cosmetic treatment is like putting lipstick on a bulldog. That's the wrong way to deal with a deteriorating situation. We can pretend everything is all right, except for one or two bad actors, or we can look more deeply at the underlying system, at how we can fix the entire system. Do we need new structures, dramatically different models? That's what leaders should be doing, taking a deeper look and offering new solutions rather than simply cosmetic responses.

Turnaround CEOs who come in to cut costs but don't rethink the business model or assumptions are making cosmetic change; they don't last. But if they rethink traditional practices, challenge underlying business assumptions, they create sustainable change. Of course, systemic change takes longer.

We're in a situation where turnarounds and quick fixes aren't enough. There's a sober mood everywhere. But, in the long run I am optimistic. I believe that if corporate citizenship and social entrepreneurship continue to flourish then we'll find new solutions.

MANFRED KETS DE VRIES: THE DARK SIDE OF LEADERSHIP

Manfred Kets de Vries is an internationally recognized expert on leadership and organizational behaviour. He is best known for his work exploring the darker side of organizational life. In particular, his pathbreaking use of psychoanalysis to understand what happens when executives derail has set him apart from his peers.

After studying economics in Holland, he completed a Doctorate in Business Administration at the Harvard Business School where he became a member of the Harvard faculty. Later, while teaching at McGill University in Canada, he retrained as a psychoanalyst, spending seven years working alongside clinical psychologists and psychiatrists – an experience that shaped his later work.

Now based at INSEAD, the international business school with campuses in France and Singapore, Kets de Vries holds the Raoul de Vitry d'Avaucourt Chair of Leadership Development. He is programme director of the top management seminar 'The Challenge of Leadership: Developing Your Emotional Intelligence'; and the programme 'Mastering Change: Developing Your Coaching and Consulting Skills'. He has received INSEAD's distinguished teacher award five times.

Professor Kets de Vries is the author, co-author or editor of 20 books, including Power and the Corporate Mind *(1975),* The Neurotic Organization *(1984), and* Organizations on the Couch *(1991). His more recent books include* Struggling with the Demon *(2001),* The Leadership Mystique *(2001), and* The Happiness Equation *(2002). A new manuscript has just been completed, entitled* Lessons on Leadership by Terror: Finding Shaka Zulu in the Attic. *He has also published over 180 scientific papers.*

A fly fishing enthusiast and member of the illustrious New York Explorer's Club, on his days off Professor Kets de Vries can be found in the rainforests or savannahs of Central Africa, the Siberian taiga, and the Arctic Circle.

He talked about why companies crave heroic leaders – and what happens when executive egos get out of control.

How would you describe your work?

Really, it is an evolution of trying to work in two main areas – management and psychoanalysis.

The first serious application of the two fields was in a book I did with Danny Miller, entitled *The Neurotic Organization*. That was the first time someone tried to show in a systematic way the relationship between personality, leadership, corporate culture and strategy.

And that gave you a distinctive slant on leadership?

I became a sort of pathologist of organizations. People would ask me to look at organizations that they thought were going in the wrong direction. So I edited a book called *Organizations on the Couch*. I'd written some books before – *Prisoners of Leadership*, *The Irrational Executive* and another called *Leaders, Fools and Imposters* – they were looking at the darker side of organizations, and particularly the darker side of leadership. How do leaders derail, what goes wrong? How can you recognize the signals when things go wrong and what can you can do about it?

In your experience, how many business leaders are well adjusted individuals?

You can argue that 20 percent of the general population is relatively healthy; 20 percent is relatively sick; and the other 60 percent somewhere in the middle. That applies to most people I meet. If you are a CEO you usually have a 'magnificent obsession' and that comes with a price. You are obsessed by certain things having to do with business. You may not have the greatest talent for other parts of your life that may result in negative side effects such as a high incidence of divorce.

But on the other hand I must admit I don't get the extreme pathological cases on my programmes. The people who apply are usually aware of many of their shortcomings. CEOs who are totally dysfunctional probably are not that interested to know more about themselves.

The real disease of many executives, CEOs in particular, is narcissism. And we have seen some abysmal examples recently – from Dennis Kozlowski at Tyco, to Kenneth Lay at Enron. Jean-Marie Messier at Vivendi was another example. That is very costly to society.

Is narcissism always destructive?

Let me put it this way, narcissism has a very bad connotation. We think of the narcissist looking in the mirror, oblivious of others. We have to realize that you need a solid dose of narcissism to be able to function properly. I tend to make a distinction between reactive and constructive narcissism.

What's the difference?

Basically, there are people who are lucky when they are growing up; they have a background of support, fairly nice parents, and they feel good in their skins and they are really pleasant people to be with. They are assertive and know what they want, but they are not totally me-oriented.

Then you have the reactive narcissists who have had a lot of trauma in their lives. Some of those reactive narcissists make a decision and say I've had a bad deal in life but I'm going to make it better for the rest of the world. The other group may suffer from the Monte Christo Complex; they want to get even. These are the people who can be exploitative, vindictive, totally self-centred, and treat others people as things rather than human beings.

They talk in abstractions about the good of mankind and the good of the organization but have no real sense of the human factor. They treat other human beings as things. There is a lack of empathy. Here I'd like to make another caveat. I have seen people who at least superficially looked like relatively decent human beings not being able to handle the position of the top job. There are certain pressures unique to that position and some people can't handle it. And as a result of that, whatever narcissistic disposition they have it starts to get overboard. So there exist a lot of varieties of reactive narcissism.

How does that destructive form of narcissism manifest itself?

Whatever it might be you see it in their behaviour. They become very me-oriented and in the end lose their sense of boundaries. Once they lose their boundary management then they start to believe that the normal rules don't apply to them any more. Kozlowski is a great example because he didn't make a distinction between what was his, and what was the organization's.

So they lose their sense of reality-testing; they just hear echoes of what they want to hear. They don't like bad news. So they don't create what you'd call a climate of healthy disrespect for the boss. They cannot tolerate a contrary atmosphere. They finally find themselves in a hall of mirrors and start to believe their own delusions. Such a situation isn't exactly ideal for effective decision-making.

But doesn't narcissism go hand in hand with the sort of charisma that is expected of leaders?

The concept of charisma comes originally from the work of Max Weber and in that context it means people who are prophets. What it is really about is that the moment you are in a leadership position, people project their fantasies onto you. So what are you going to do? Are you going to use these projected fantasies, or are you not going to use them? Furthermore, are you going to use these fantasies for the good or for the bad?

So what you're saying is that charisma is largely in the eye of the beholder?

It's a fantasy. But I must admit if you want to stimulate such a fantasy you can do a few things. It helps if you have rhetorical skills – if you are a good orator. It helps if you can tell stories, and know how to use strong imagery – God and country is not bad imagery to use. I am referring to the domain of symbol manipulation. It helps if you have a good memory for names and can mention people by their names; if you are able to single them out. It helps if you are attentive and people have at least the illusion that you listen to them. Charismatic people often have that gift, which I call the Teddy Bear factor – they make people feel comfortable. It also helps if you are willing to ask questions and challenge the status quo – if you engage people in dialogue. Furthermore, your charismatic appeal increases if you can dramatize the risk. Here the David against Goliath symbolism can be very useful.

So, can someone be an effective leader without charisma?

Sure. But I strongly believe that to be an effective leader you need a certain dose of self-awareness. One element of the self-awareness is realizing what you're not good at, or what you do not like to do. When you reach the stage of being a senior executive, it's better to work on your strengths than to work on your weaknesses.

Effective leaders will create an executive role constellation in which other people will compensate for their weaknesses. If you are a fairly low-key executive but there are situations where you need to be able to put a crate of beer on the table and rally the troops, you call on someone else in senior management to help you with it.

People have been talking about the demise of heroic leadership for years. Do you see any evidence of that?

It's nonsense. The heroic leader will never die because we need them. It's part of human nature, part of the human condition. And this is particularly the case when people are exposed to discontinuous change.

Change makes people anxious. And anxious people look for someone to calm them down – what can be called the containment element of leadership. So we are always looking for leaders who can do that. And the press usually does everything they can do to reinforce this image of strong leaders who can act as saviours.

But heroes often end up becoming villains?

Nobody can live up to those expectations of the press; this myth creation. So eventually all these leaders are a disappointment. It's fascinating if you look at the covers of *Fortune* and *Businessweek* over the years how many of those people have been shot down. So the press creates them and the press kills them. I always say the moment you get on the cover of *Fortune* or *Businessweek* it's the beginning of the end.

You start to believe your own press and you start to suffer from what the Greeks called 'hubris' – excessive pride. And like the mythical Icarus who flew too close to the sun, you also may tumble down. So there's a bit of a paradox. I sometimes ask people in class how many of you are charismatic? No one of course raises their hand. But in a way, anyone can be charismatic. It's a bit like the Chancey Gardner syndrome in the Peter Sellers film *Being There*, which has this illiterate gardener who eventually ends up as a candidate for the presidency. People just project their fantasies onto him.

And that's true across cultures? Not just a western thing – the American John Wayne syndrome?

No. It is stronger in the individualistic cultures, but the Japanese have their heroes, too – it all depends on the situation.

What is happening at the moment which is the swing of the pendulum in all cultures is the shift from the heroic leader on the cover of *Fortune* magazine to the subtle leader.

At this point in time, after all the noise about the hero leader, we are looking for the quiet leader. So the subtle leaders come to the fore, and before we know it, they (helped by the press) also become heroic leaders; that's the great irony so the pendulum keeps on swinging.

JOHN KOTTER: IN THE FIELD

While some of his Harvard Business School colleagues are prolific contributors to the Harvard Business Review, John Kotter has written only six articles. At first sight, it seems a slender basis for an academic career. But Kotter's timing has been impeccable. His ideas have struck a chord. Kotter was on the leadership trail at the right time. Then it was change management. Then culture. Then careers. If success was measured in article reprints, Kotter is a success. Then there are his bestselling books, Leading Change, Corporate Culture and Performance, *and* A Force for Change. *Managers feel that he understands them. So much so that one speaker's bureau quotes Professor Kotter's speaking fee as starting at $75,000.*

And yet, Kotter is the archetypal career academic. He celebrated 30 years at Harvard in 2002 and was among the youngest Harvard faculty members ever given tenure and a full professorship. He talks about how he manages to make the right connections with what is happening in the workplace.

How do you work?

The simple logic of my work is that I am a pure field guy. I hang around talking to people. I talk to managers. I sit and watch them. I snoop around, listen to their problems. It's simple detective work. My work is developed by looking out of the window at what's going on. It is about seeing patterns. If I'm good at anything it's pattern analysis and thinking through the implications of those patterns.

What are you working on now?

My last book was a biography of Konosuke Matsushita who no one, in the United States at least, knew anything about. Some big insights came out of that which I'm still working through. Now I'm working on *Leading Change 2 – Leading Change* came out in 1996 – which is a more tactical book than its predecessor. It is told in the first person by people struggling through change.

So you have adopted a more personal tone?

> Through my speaking I have become more aware of the power of stories. I use stories constantly – 95 per cent of what I do is storytelling. It has evolved as I've thought about it as a process of education.

What are your stories drawn from?

> There's no one who has spent more time talking to managers. That's one reason why my books have won awards. I spend a huge amount of time talking to people.

Is that worth more than theorizing?

> Who would write a better book about trees: someone in the forest or someone in an office?

You have written about change and the importance of a mobilizing, inspiring vision. Is that possible in an environment marked by downsizing?

> It is not easy, but it is both possible and necessary. The key is to go beyond the downsizing clichés – talking only of lean and nice. And, carefree statements like 'I see a smaller firm in the future' are not a vision that allows people to see a light at the end of the tunnel, that mobilizes people, or that makes them endure sacrifices.

So, what's your advice?

> Be creative, be genuine, and most of all, know why you're doing what you're doing. Communicate that and the organization will be stronger. Anything short of this will breed the cynicism that results when we see inconsistencies between what people say and what they do, between talk and practice.

Can a single person ignite true change?

> The desire for change may start with one person – the Lee Iacocca, Sam Walton, or Lou Gerstner. But it certainly doesn't end there. Nobody can provoke great changes alone. There are people that think it is possible, but it is not true. Successful change requires the efforts of a critical mass of key individuals – a group of 2–50 people,

depending on the size of the corporation we are considering – in order to move the organization in significantly different directions. If the minimum of critical mass is not reached in the first stages, nothing really important will happen.

Failing to establish a sense of urgency is one of the key mistakes made by change leaders. In Leading Change you discuss seven additional steps in successful change efforts.

That's right. Beyond establishing a sense of urgency, organizations need to create a powerful, guiding coalition, develop vision and strategy, communicate the change vision, empower broad-based action, celebrate short-term wins, continuously reinvigorate the initiative with new projects and participants, and anchor the change in the corporate culture.

What does this 'guiding coalition' look like?

The guiding coalition needs to have four characteristics. First, it needs to have position power. The group needs to consist of a combination of individuals who, if left out of the process, are in positions to block progress. Second, expertise. The group needs a variety of skills, perspectives, experiences, and so forth relative to the project. Third, credibility. When the group announces initiatives will its members have reputations that get the ideas taken seriously? And fourth, leadership. The group needs to be composed of proven leaders. And remember, in all of this the guiding coalition should not be assumed to be composed exclusively of managers. Leadership is found throughout the organization, and it's leadership you want – not management.

Who needs to be avoided when building this team?

Individuals with large egos – and those I call 'snakes.' The bigger the ego, the less space there is for anyone else to think and work. And snakes are individuals who destroy trust. They spread rumours, talk about other group members behind their backs, nod yes in meetings but condemn project ideas as unworkable or short-sighted when talking with colleagues. Trust is critical in successful change efforts, and these two sorts of individuals put trust in jeopardy.

'Communication' seems to crop up in most discussions of organizational effectiveness, and certainly in discussions of effective change. What do you mean when you use the term?

Effectively communicating the change vision is critical to success. This should seem obvious, yet for some reason, executives tend to stop communicating during change, when in actuality they should be communicating more than ever. Effective change communication is both verbal and nonverbal. It includes simplicity, communicating via different types of forums and over various channels, leading by example – which is very important – and two-way communication. Change is stressful for everyone. This is the worst possible time for executives to close themselves off from contact with employees. And this is particularly important if short-term sacrifices are necessary, including firing people.

Who were your mentors?

There were Paul Lawrence and Tony Athos at Harvard, and the social psychologist Ed Schein at MIT. They all took an interest in me. After that, you collect ideas.

Have you ever thought about working for an organization?

It has never crossed my mind for a nanosecond.

How about creating an organization?

At most I've had one or two employees. I've thought about building an organization, but it's not necessarily what I'm good at doing.

Have you ever thought about working elsewhere? 30 years with one organization is a long time.

If your business is education, Boston is not a bad place to be with Harvard, MIT and its various universities.

But you are involved in a number of companies.

I'm investing in a company in the e-learning area. E-learning is going to be the biggest thing since Guttenberg. It will take wisdom and ideas and make them available to the many. Access to wisdom will go up by a factor of thousands. As an educator I've been exploring the possibilities. It's great fun to watch it develop from its infancy and try to develop your own vision.

You work in a highly competitive field. Who do you see as your competitors?

If you do well at what you do and it makes an impact, you don't think in competitive terms. Are you happy with your contribution? When you fail to meet your own expectations then you start thinking in terms of competition.

DANIEL GOLEMAN: MAXED EMOTIONS

Daniel Goleman is one of the most influential thinkers to hit the business world in recent years. The bearded psychologist and former journalist has spread the gospel of emotional intelligence to a largely grateful business world. It is based on the notion that the ability of managers to understand and manage their own emotions and relationships is the key to better business performance.

His 1997 book, Emotional Intelligence, *has more than five million copies in print and was on the* New York Times *bestseller list for 18 months. His follow-up book,* Working With Emotional Intelligence *applied his ideas to the business world, and became an immediate bestseller.*

His book Primal Leadership *makes the case for cultivating emotionally intelligent leaders. In it, Goleman and co-authors Richard E. Boyatzis and Annie McKee explore how the four domains of emotional intelligence – self-awareness, self-management, social awareness and relationship management – give rise to different styles of leadership. These constitute a leadership repertoire, which enlightened leaders can master to maximize their effectiveness.*

Goleman is both a clinical psychologist and a distinguished journalist. He has received two Pulitzer Prize nominations for his articles in the New York Times. *He works with companies through the emotional intelligence practice of the Hay Group. He is also co-chairman of the Consortium for Social and Emotional Learning in the Workplace, based in the School of Professional Psychology at Rutgers University, which recommends best practices for developing emotional competence.*

Emotional intelligence isn't a new phenomenon, it's always been there. So why has it become so important in today's business world?

It has always been a factor in success individually, particularly in business, but that fact hasn't been clearly identified until recently. Two things: there's been a convergence of forces that have called it to collective attention. One is the fact that in the last ten years, there's been a critical mass of research in science – brain science and behavioural science – that makes clear that there is capacity called emotional intelligence.

The notion itself was articulated first in 1990 so it's quite a new notion. Two Yale psychologists first came up with the term emotional intelligence: Peter Salovey and John Mayer. They wrote an article in what frankly was a very obscure psychology journal, but I was a journalist at the *New York Times* and my beat was brain and behavioural science, and one of the things I did was to scour the scientific literature looking for important new findings and concepts, and I thought that was an extremely important concept. I went on to write the book about it.

Meanwhile, companies had been doing internal studies, quite independent of the notion of emotional intelligence, looking at what distinguished star performers in a given field – say, the head of a division or a sales team. They compared them to people at the mean who were just average performers, trying to distinguish and distil the specific abilities that were found consistently in stars that you didn't see in others and then trying to hire people or promote people, or develop people for those abilities. And when I wrote the book *Working with Emotional Intelligence* and then my recent book *Primal Leadership: Realizing the Power of Emotional Intelligence* (co-authored with Richard E. Boyatzis and Annie McKee and published in 2002 in the US by Harvard Business School Press), I was able to harvest hundreds of studies like that which had been done individually and independently for different organizations or looking at different roles within organizations – most of which were proprietary.

When I aggregated that data, what I found was that abilities like, for example, being able to manage your disturbing emotions (keeping them from disabling your ability to function) or empathy (being able to perceive how people were feeling and seeing things from their perspective) or the ability to co-operate well on a team – which are based on emotional intelligence – were the preponderance of the abilities that distinguished the best from the worst. And so there was this independent database that showed that emotional intelligence was extremely important in this context.

How do you score on your own EI measures? Are you emotionally intelligent?

Everyone has a profile of strengths and weaknesses. My own profile is, like anyone else's, rather uneven. But to get the most accurate, honest answer you'd have to ask the people who have worked with me – and my wife.

Is there a pattern: do women tend to score higher for example?

When you look at gender differences you're looking at basically overlapping bell curves – there are more similarities than differences between the genders. But the differences that do emerge are that women tend to score better than men on average at empathy and some relationship abilities. Men tend to score better than women on emotional self-management and self-confidence. So I think each gender has its own strengths.

How much of EI is already determined before adulthood?

The roots of each of these abilities start early in life. Every competence that distinguishes an outstanding leader in business has a developmental history, and if you ask people – and studies have been done – how did you become such a good team leader, for example, it will always start with a story, typically in middle school years at around 11, 12 or 13. This is a real story. A woman who is a fantastic team leader was asked when did this first start and she said she moved to a new school and didn't know anyone so she thought she could meet people by joining the field hockey team. And it turned out she wasn't such a good player but was very good at teaching the new kids the game. So she became a sort of de facto assistant coach. Then it turned out in her first job after university that she was in sales and no one showed her the ropes, so when she learned them she spontaneously started teaching new people on the sales team. And she was so good at it that the company made a video about her and that led to the fast track that resulted in her finally becoming senior VP for sales. So each one of these abilities is learned and learned over the course of life, and articulated, refined and sharpened as you go up the ladder. That's an important point.

Are business leaders more emotionally intelligent today than in the past? How does EI relate to what others perceive as charisma?

It's about as uneven as it ever was, frankly. One reason is that although there's clear data that these abilities matter, it doesn't mean that companies always use that to make decisions about who should be promoted. When it comes to who should be a leader we are still prone to the Peter Principle – people being promoted to their level of incompetence. The most common error isn't that you're promoted because of the old boy network, which is the old story. The new story is that people tend to be promoted to leadership today because of technical expertise. You're a very good individual performer, and the automatic but mistaken assumption is made that of course you'll then be very good at leading a team of people like yourself. But the fallacy there is that what made you a good individual performer – your technical expertise – actually has nothing to do with what distinguishes people who are good team leaders. And the business world is rife with that. At the *New York Times* I saw it all the time. Journalists who were outstanding as journalists would become heads of desks or editors, which they were often terrible at.

What's the relationship between emotional intelligence and charisma? Presumably, charisma is partly in the eye of the beholder, and partly to do with certain skills that people project?

Charisma in terms of this model has to do with the ability of persuasion and communication. Bill Clinton is a beautiful example of someone who is fantastic at both empathy and persuasion, which builds on empathy. If you meet Bill Clinton or are with him you feel like you're the most important person in the world to him at that moment. He really tunes in. And he uses what he perceives in order to translate that into the language that will communicate most powerfully with you. Charismatic leaders do that with groups as a whole and he certainly did. But you can also use him to illustrate that everyone has a profile of strengths and weaknesses in this domain. Because when it came to impulse control, he really flunked.

The other side of that is that as people become more emotionally competent, isn't there a danger that they become more Machiavellian?

Only in rare cases because Machiavellian behaviour – which is where you take your self-interest over and above every other goal, so basically you'll do anything to get ahead – is a lapse in several emotional intelligence competencies, one of which is integrity. Another has to do with being able to co-operate well in a group. People who are Machiavellian, in other words who get a short-term gain, do it at a cost to other people. They leave a legacy of resentment, ill-feeling, and anger, which very often catches up with them later in their career.

One aspect of narcissistic people is that they often lack empathy, and yet we still seem to want these people as leaders. Or perhaps we need it to get on?

I don't know that we do anymore. The most compelling data on that has to do with leadership style, the emotional climate the leader creates, and how that in turn translates into the motivation and ability of people to work at their best. The data looks like this: the people who are, for example, visionary, who can articulate a shared mission in a way that motivates and inspires people, create a very positive emotional climate, as do leaders who are very good listeners who take a true interest in the individuals who work for them and try to understand what they want for their career and how they can help them along. So do leaders who know that having a good time together builds emotional capital for when the pressure is on. All of those styles create the kind of climate where people can work at their best.

However, the leader who is the distant narcissist, the kind of command-and-control, do-it-because-I-say-so leader actually creates a very negative emotional climate. Especially if they become the kind of narcissistic leader who feels not only are they right, but who then blows up at people, gets extremely impatient, hypercritical and so on, which is a danger of that style. And that poisons the climate and alienates people. You lose talent and people end up spending more time thinking about the boss and complaining about him than doing their work.

I'm not sure the data today supports the kind of mandate and power that we've given bosses like that in the past.

A particular area of interest to us is the genesis of big business ideas. Where did your ideas about EI come from?

The biggest influence on my thinking was my mentor at Harvard, the late David McClelland (1917–1998), who, in the early 1970s when I was a graduate student there working with him, wrote an article that at the time was a very radical proposal. He wrote it in the *American Psychologist*, the main psychology journal in the US. He said if you want to hire the best person for a job don't look at their academic grades, don't look at their test scores, don't look at their IQ, don't look at some personality profile, don't look at their connections, their social class, and certainly don't look at their letters of recommendation. He said what you should first do is look at the people within your own organization who have held that post in the past and been outstanding at it and systematically compare them with the people who have held the post and done poorly or average. And then determine what made the best so good and hire people with those capabilities. That is the basis for the methodology now called competence modelling, which was the data I harvested when I wrote *The New Leaders* and *Working with Emotional Intelligence*.

So, he's had certainly the most direct influence both in showing me a method for having an informed answer to the question of what makes someone a truly good leader; and also in making it possible 20 or 30 years later for me to harvest information from literally hundreds of organizations around the world.

What about Howard Gardner's work?

Howard Gardner who was a grad student with me at Harvard in those days, and a personal friend who also opened a door for me when he proposed the model of multiple intelligences, which says that in different domains there are different kinds of abilities that can be called an intelligence over and above the standard IQ model which dates from the early twentieth century and is a narrow achievement model – just verbal and maths abilities, and a few spatial abilities. He argued that in every domain where there are competencies created and valued, there is a specific kind of intelligence. So, for example, there is a musical intelligence, there's a kinaesthetic intelligence in the domain of sports, ballet and so on. And he also said there are personal intelligences and it's that domain of the personal intelligence that I've unpacked in explaining emotional intelligence.

Are IQ tests obsolete now?

No. IQ tests are very broad indicators of the fields that a person can qualify for, where a person can enter and hold a job in. The problem with IQ tests is they don't go the next step. So, let's say you're managing a pool of engineers in your corporation, or R&D scientists, or accountants, lawyers, or whatever, IQ tests do not predict who among that pool of people now in the field itself will distinguish themselves over time as the most successful, the most effective, the most productive – whatever your measure of success is. It's interesting, even in the sciences, IQ does not predict who over the course of a career will emerge as the most eminent scientist. Other abilities do and they turn out to be the emotional intelligence abilities. So in other words, IQ is a threshold ability for a field but it is not a distinguishing ability, and I'm most interested in the distinguishing abilities. IQ is a very good indicator, however, of what field you could enter.

Thomas Stewart is another journalist who became a guru by taking obscure academic ideas and translating them so that the business world can understand their message. How much do you think your journalistic skills have helped you?

I think they were invaluable because I was trained as a psychologist and frankly, when I entered journalism I was the slow kid on the block. My first job in journalism I had a very kindly managing editor and after I'd write an article in typical journalese – I don't mean journalism, I mean typical academic journal style, which is Latinate, passive voice, absolutely flat prose – he would go through it literally line by line and word by word and show me how to change it to make it lively and engaging, and make every word count and to eliminate 80 per cent of the words I had chosen. And he transformed my writing style. And I think my time at a daily newspaper at the *New York Times* just gave me more and more practice at a style that was engaging. Meanwhile, I was able to use my expertise in psychology to go into the academic literature and search for ideas that really did have impact and should have a wider audience. Those two things in combination gave me the abilities to write the book *Emotional Intelligence*.

You say that emotional intelligence can be developed. So what practical things can managers do to develop those abilities?

Yes. First of all, organizations can set up a format and make accessible a mode of learning that is appropriate to the emotional intelligence domain. What I mean by that is you don't improve these abilities in the same way that you learn technical expertise like how to do a certain computer program, nor in the mode that you learned when you went to school. It's a different part of the brain that's involved. And it doesn't learn as quickly as the neo-cortex. The model actually is skill acquisition. If there's something you're not as good at as you'd like to be, you can improve, that's the good news, but you need to do it in a way that brings along this part of the brain. Firstly, you have to care. It has to be something you are motivated about. It has to be something that really matters to you because if you don't you won't make the necessary effort and it's going to take some months. Now, it doesn't take any extra time because you use your day-to-day encounters as the opportunities to practise and hone the improved mode.

So, for example, to take a common problem, you don't listen well. Someone walks into your office and you start telling them what you think, rather than first hearing what they have to say and making sure you understand it. Well, that's a choice point that you can choose to make an effort to change and instead of just jumping in and giving your opinion you can make sure that you really have heard and understood. If you do that at every opportunity, what will happen is that slowly you're going to be building a new neural network, you are strengthening connections between brain cells so that your former default setting at the neural level which was to jump in, now has an alternate path. You're strengthening the circuitry there. And there will come a day when you automatically sit back and listen to understand before you give your opinion – which means that that alternate circuit has become the new default option, it's now the stronger pathway in the brain.

That kind of learning has been used successfully by Richard Boyatzis at Case Western University School of Management. He's been doing it with his executive MBAs for 10 or 15 years. He's done follow-ups with them in their work where he asks other people to evaluate them on the behaviour they tried to improve back in their MBA programme and he's found that if you use this mode of learning, you can see the improvements seven years later – that's as long as he's done it. That's quite remarkable. Most business seminars or weekend seminars, or even a week off-site – if that's all you do, it won't be enough to make the requisite change. You really do need the sustained learning opportunity.

How does your message go down in India or China?

Interestingly, I'm travelling to India again tomorrow. India is hugely taken with emotional intelligence. I must get several emails daily – weekly if not daily – from India, from people who have read the book and want to apply it either in their graduate work or in the management of their companies.

China is a slightly different story. The last talk I gave in China was arranged by the government of Shanghai talking to business leaders in the Shanghai community. Because of their entry into the WTO, Chinese leaders are realizing that they need to update their management abilities and skills to a world class standard. So, even though one of the things I'm talking about is shifting from a rather totalitarian control style which was the pervasive style through China, to a more democratic style where leaders motivate, listen and so on, they've been extremely receptive because they realize that to compete in the world market with multinationals that are already using these styles of leadership, they are going to have to make the shift themselves. So China, to my surprise, is actually quite receptive.

Interestingly, Chinese business has always valued relationships and networks. Companies in the US and the UK have spent recent decades trying to squeeze all emotion out of the workplace.

That was a rather foolish endeavour because we don't ever leave our emotions at home when we go to work. They were always there; they were just squelched or ignored – sometimes at disastrous cost. Most Asian cultures are quite relationship-oriented and business has always been based on relationships as you say, which means many of these skills are natural in the culture. On the other hand, India, perhaps because it was a British colony, had very strong command and control structures among the business class. But most businesses, even large corporations, are family-owned businesses even today. And the culture was similar to that in China but for different historical reasons. So they both need to make the shift. On the other hand, the way you do business – as opposed to the structure of the company, but how people, especially entrepreneurs, do business – is very relationship-oriented so a number of these skills come quite naturally.

Tell me about your relationship with the Hay Group?

David McLennen, along with being a professor, started a consulting firm called McBerr which became part of the Hay Group. So, when I was working with emotional intelligence in the business setting, I was looking for a business partner because I knew there would be demand created and I wanted to be able to recommend someone in good conscience where people could get these practices I was talking about. I did that in two ways. One was to form a business alliance with the Hay Group. The second was to co-found a consortium based at Rutgers University which supports the best practices in the field so they could be widely disseminated.

It's a financial relationship?

It's a financial relationship with Hay, mainly around the 360-degree methodology I co-designed with Richard Boyatzis. They distribute it and we collect royalties on it. That's the main business relationship at this point. On the other hand, the Hay Group is doing a good job of bringing these methods on. But I would also say there are other groups worldwide, if they are following the best practice standards you see on that Web site, that are offering the same services.

If there is one message from more recent work that is different to your other books, what would it be?

That businesses need to pay attention to the role of emotional intelligence in outstanding leaders, and to build it into their culture and systems. Not just to pay lip service to it and certainly not to ignore it, but to actually make it a part of their standard operating procedure, and to make it clear that they are hiring for these abilities, and promoting people for them and they are serious about helping people develop further strengths in this area.

Does emotional intelligence in leaders provide any protection against the sorts of excesses we have seen in the corporate world of late, Enron etc.?

One of the fundamental capabilities that distinguishes emotionally intelligent leaders from others is integrity. Business needs to make a pendulum swing from a culture where whatever is legal and whatever accounting would approve was done – that is, a culture where it is very hard to raise ethical concerns to one where ethics becomes a business advantage. That requires leaders who are ethical, and that has always been a part of the emotional intelligence model.

You wrote the introduction to the book Business: The Ultimate Resource. In it you talk about business intelligence – is that a bringing together of different strands such as emotional intelligence and others?

In the introduction to *Business: The Ultimate Resource*, I consider the question of whether there might be a business intelligence that is broader than emotional intelligence, which includes not just the competencies I've been talking about but also goes through to those of technical expertise and cognitive abilities as the widest definition of what it is that makes someone good at business, no matter what part of business they may be dealing with.

One thing that this book has done is to level the playing field in a quite interesting manner. For years, Robert Kelley at Carnegie-Mellon University has been asking people who work in a wide variety of companies the same question: what percentage of the knowledge you need to do your job is stored in your own mind? Back in the mid-1980s, the answer was typically around 75 per cent, but by the turn of the millennium, that percentage had slid to as low as 15 per cent. This change reflects the sheer rate of growth in the amount of information available. More knowledge has been generated in the past century, it is said, than in all history before – and the rate of increase is accelerating. And another piece of data, the star performers in business, it turns out, are four times faster than people who are average at gaining access to new expertise.

It's quite extraordinary. For that Monday morning meeting when you need to know about team management or turning leads into sales, something that you have just not had experience of, you now have a way of quickly studying up without having to rummage through a business library to find a text about it, and in that sense it levels the playing field.

How does it go down in a tractor plant in Nebraska where people aren't used to hearing about the more touchy-feely stuff?

It's not touchy-feely, that's a misconception. This is being intelligent *about* emotions, not being emotional. I'm not saying that people should necessarily express emotions openly and fluently. I'm saying that you should be able to manage your distressing emotions so that they don't get in the way of the work you have to do. And you need to do that because there is a relationship between the emotional centres of the brain that pump out your distressing emotions and the neo-cortex, pre-frontal brain, which needs to take in information and understand it clearly and respond flexibly. The more you are under the sway of the emotional centres, the less nimble and the more paralysed your thinking brain becomes. So, it's because of that reciprocal relationship that you need to be able to manage emotions. And you need to be able to manage relationships effectively too. That goes down just fine in Nebraska. If you say let's be touchy-feely then you are not talking about what I'm talking about. I wouldn't even mention it in Nebraska.

Where can your ideas make the biggest impact? Is it at the sales interface or in the boardroom?

At every level where leadership is operating. So it could be at the team level, among the team members – in fact there is such a thing as team emotional intelligence. A woman named Vanessa Druskat (assistant professor of organizational behaviour at the Weatherhead School of Management) has shown that these same abilities operate at the collective level in a team and distinguish high performance teams from low performance teams. It's distributed. So, anywhere that people need to work together in order to achieve a collective goal, it is required.

Section 2
SELLING THE FUTURE

Business seers tend to dislike the term 'futurist' in the same way management gurus dislike the word 'guru'. 'Futurist' is suggestive of wacky guesswork rather than considered extrapolations from current trends. For example, John Naisbitt, author of *Megatrends*, thinks of himself as a social forecaster, and not a futurist. 'There's a lot of nonsense under the "futurist" banner,' he says.

While many claim to see the future, only a chosen few do so with perception or precision. The clarity achieved by the best is startling. Take some of the more prescient thinkers active in the 1960s. In *The Temporary Society* (1968), an underrated masterpiece of futuristic literature, Warren Bennis and Philip Slater argue that organizational forms need to harness innovation and creativity. With the Cold War then at its peak, they foresaw the collapse of Communism and sounded the death knell for bureaucracy. The duo envisioned 'temporary' organizations, teams drawing on specialists to focus on specific projects and were talking about the world of free agency long before *Fast Company* magazine was even a business plan.

Equally knowing is the *The Age of Discontinuity* by Peter Drucker, the éminence grise of management thinking. More than 20 years after its 1968 publication, Richard Pascale noted in *Managing on the Edge* that Drucker's work 'describes the commercial era in which we live'. In his book, Drucker introduces the concept of 'knowledge management'. Instead of obedient adherents to the corporate code, organizations would be populated by executives with a keen sense of their own worth – financial, intellectual, and professional. Knowledge management required the acknowledgment of the needs and aspirations of a new breed of knowledge workers.

Another tour de force was Alvin Toffler's 1970 book, *Future Shock*. Its messages were not easily contemplated by managers raised on a diet of certainty. *Future Shock* suggested that businesses were going to restructure themselves repeatedly. That would require a reduction in hierarchy and the adoption of what he called 'adhocracy'. To managers reared on command-and-control, it sounded highly implausible. After decades of assembling ornate bureaucracies and carefully constructed hierarchies, companies saw no reason to dismantle them.

Bennis, Slater, Drucker, Toffler, and a select few others, accurately predicted the uncertainties of the contemporary business world. It took time, but aside from not anticipating some events, such as the competitive emergence of Japan, they were largely right. These futurists looked into the far distance with all the grandiose bravado of explorers. The future was out there, a great big adventure. Think of the perennially quotable glimpses offered by Marshall McLuhan, who anticipated globalism and the all-encompassing grip of the media decades ago.

Now, however, time has shrunk – and so, too, has certainty. Economic transformation, social change, industrial organization – all have accelerated, so much so that confidently looking into the future is increasingly a thing of the past. Tumultuous technological progress means that today's students of the future have been reined in.

Increasingly, futurists find themselves under pressure to report on and try to make sense of the present, to peer around the corner rather than gaze into the distance. In the maelstrom of hyper-competition and frenetic change, this is understandable. Companies and executives want to make sense of the here and now to secure tomorrow's advantage. They don't want blue-sky thinking when there are real rain clouds gathering overhead. Futurism has become a form of arbitrage – an attempt to profit from small differences in the current outlook. Yet while it is true that things are happening so rapidly in the business world that venturing an opinion on 'what might be' appears an act of futility and folly, at its best, futurism is not a protective measure but a bold act of exploration.

When Herman Kahn published *The Emerging Japanese Superstate: Challenge and Response* in 1970, his views ran counter to received wisdom. He was right – and then right again with *The Coming Boom: Economic, Political, and Social*, which anticipated, during a seemingly endless recession, America's recovery. The bravest futurists are those that put their reputations on the line. Long may they continue to do so.

PETER SCHWARTZ: THINKING THE UNTHINKABLE

An internationally renowned futurist, Peter Schwartz is a leading advocate of scenario planning – a technique that helps organizations 'think the unthinkable' by creating alternative stories, or scenarios, about how the future might pan out. His 1991 bestseller The Art of the Long View *introduced the concept and vocabulary of scenarios to companies around the world.*

For a futurist, Schwartz has an impressive past. Before joining Royal Dutch/Shell in London, he was the director of the Strategic Environment Center at SRI International, one of Silicon Valley's most prodigious research centres. At Shell, he was mentored by Pierre Wack, the company's celebrated head of planning, and from 1982 to 1986 he was head of scenario planning. Under Schwartz's leadership, Shell's scenario planners had some notable successes. In 1982, for example, they speculated that oil prices could collapse to $16 a barrel. They also foresaw the collapse of the Soviet Union years before it happened.

In 1987, Schwartz co-founded GBN (Global Business Network), which specializes in helping organizations apply scenario planning. Now part of the Monitor Consulting Group, GBN's clients include many Fortune 500 companies, the US defense research agency DARPA (Defense Advanced Research Projects Agency) and the CIA. He has also written a string of influential books and articles, including When Good Companies Do Bad Things *– co-authored with Blair Gibb. Co-authored with Pete Leyden, his most recent book* The Long Boom *predicted a 25 year period of uninterrupted economic growth and prosperity. The subsequent recession appears to disprove his theory.*

Schwartz has also worked as a script consultant on a number of films, including Deep Impact, War Games, *and* Sneakers. *He assembled a team of futurists to envision the world in 2058 for Steven Spielberg's latest film* Minority Report.

Peter Schwartz talked about the evolution of scenario thinking.

How would you describe yourself? Consultant, writer, speaker?

Yes, yes and yes. I do all of the above and I'm also a venture capitalist. The way I really think of myself is as someone who helps organizations think about the future.

How did you get involved with making the film* Minority Report*?

I had worked on several films before and GBN had worked on another one for Dreamworks a few years ago called *Deep Impact*. So when Spielberg wanted to do *Minority Report*, the first thing they did was call us and say 'can you help us create the future'. We assembled a team of 20 people and spent three days in a hotel with Steven and the art director. We wrote the bible for the movie. If you see the film all the technical details, except the core story which was by Philip K. Dick, came from us

Is scenario planning more relevant to the post-September 11 world?

Thinking the unthinkable has become a useful idea again. The magnitude of change, the shock, in the short-run and the long-run that such an event could happen, is quite profound. It has put uncertainty back on the table in a big way.

We've seen this reflected in our business. Since September 11, a lot of consulting companies have had trouble; we have not.

In the 1940s, Herman Kahn at the Rand Corporation used scenario planning to explore potential nuclear war scenarios. But could anyone have predicted September 11?

It was the most predicted event in history. It was predicted by so many people – myself included I might add. Osama Bin Laden said he was going to do it. And he did what he said he was going to do.

We wrote for the Rudman Commission, (Hart-Rudman Commission into US national security in the 21st century) that the forces of Bin Laden and Al Qaeda would fly a jumbo jet into the World Trade Center and major buildings in Washington. We weren't the first or the only ones who said that. A number of people said it. If you just read what Bin Laden said and looked at the history and his behaviour. He went after the World Trade Center before, and he comes back for his targets if he doesn't get them.

So this was the easiest thing in the world to predict. You couldn't know that it would be on September 11 but you could know it was coming. Over the course of the summer there were lots of signals that something big was about to happen, and this is the thing that he was most visibly planning.

Have the risks increased for business?

The risks have become greater. It's not just a matter of perception, it is real. The threat of war, the threat of conflict and that disruption is very real.

How has scenario planning evolved from the Rand Corporation in the 1940s to Shell in the 1970s through to the present day?

First of all there is a recognition that big complicated methodologies and elaborate computer models are not the optimal way. It has moved away from formal planning-like processes more toward a thinking tool. And it's not much more profound than that. So it's a methodology for contingent thinking, for thinking about different possibilities and asking the question, 'what if?'

So it's more an art than a science?

Absolutely. That's why I called my book *The Art of the Long View*. The second thing that is quite important is it has moved away from a focus on the external world toward the internal world of the executive. This was Pierre Wack's big insight at Shell. The objective is not to get a more accurate picture of the world around us but to influence decision-making inside the mind of the decision-maker. The objective of good scenarios is better decisions, not better predictions.

How easy is it for someone in India or China where there is a paucity of good information to generate useful scenarios?

I was just in China a few weeks ago and they have now begun serious efforts at that kind of contingent thinking. I don't know about India. Singapore is a very active practitioner of scenario planning. Quite a lot has been done in Thailand and Malaysia. We just worked with the national oil company of Malaysia, Petronas – they were introducing scenario planning. In much of Asia this notion has begun to take hold.

Presumably though the quality of the information you feed in affects the quality of the scenarios?

What's interesting about China is that things are really changing.

The government tries to block people getting access but they're not very successful. They don't fight too hard, and if you don't make yourself too obnoxious you actually have access to very good information. There's no question that the quality of the information you use has an enormous impact on the quality of the results. Good information is essential. That said it's harder to do this in places like Saudi Arabia.

Do different sets of people come up with the same scenarios given the same information?

We just tried that experiment a few weeks ago for the first time. We had two back-to-back scenario groups both looking at political scenarios for the world. One was all non-Americans, the other was all Americans, to see if they came up with different views of the world and they did – quite strikingly so. We did the non-Americans first and then the Americans and about two-thirds of the way through we showed them the non-American results, and had them react to that as well.

What were the big differences?

The overwhelming message was the antipathy non-Americans now feel towards the US. And Americans just weren't seeing that at all. There was no war on terrorism anywhere outside the US. In fact, there was a clear perception that the US was the problem. The scenario that everyone else was talking about was how could you constrain the US, not how could you defeat terrorism. So there are completely different perceptions of the world.

And you also do scenario planning with the CIA?

Yes. We've been working with them now for about six or seven years.

This is new. They consciously didn't do multiple scenarios. They were asked to do only one scenario and, of course, this always led them to be surprised because they always came up with the least surprising scenario by definition.

The most probable is more of the same. Therefore, you always throw out the outlying scenarios – like there will be an Iranian revolution, Haiti will collapse, or that the Soviet Union will go away – big one. But now that's changed.

Your book When Good Companies Do Bad Things *looked at corporate ethics. On a scale of one to ten, how seriously has the reputation of corporate America been damaged by Enron and other recent scandals?*

Ten. It is a really big deal – both domestically and globally. Domestically there's been a tremendous loss of faith and we see it reflected in the stock market – quite understandably. Globally, there is an undermining of US stature around the world because we have been pressing the notion of free markets, capitalism, big corporations and so on, and saying that it creates jobs and prosperity and so on. Now we find that a number of major US corporations were dishonest. I think that will take a long time to come back.

What happened to The Long Boom you predicted?

Some parts of it have persisted and some have changed. The Long Boom was predicated on two big ideas, one of which is still right, the other of which has been fundamentally challenged. The first was massive technological change driving productivity growth and new industries. That idea is still right. The other idea is now much more open to challenge and that is the idea of globalization bringing many more people into the global economy. We've seen both a political push back against globalization in the streets of Seattle, and Genoa and elsewhere, and the disruptions caused by the events of September 11, and we've had a US administration that is less interested in globalization and more interested in global domination. And so, as a result, the political process has moved against globalization. Now we have to consider whether that will continue.

Is the world becoming more uncertain?

The world has always been uncertain. If it seemed less uncertain before, it was only in appearance. It has always been really uncertain. It was, is, and will be.

WATTS WACKER: FRINGE BENEFITS

Futurist Watts Wacker is the chief executive of the consulting, research, training firm and new age think-tank, FirstMatter (www.firstmatter.com). Wacker describes himself as a twenty-first century alchemist as well as 'a cross between James Brown and the unknown comic – the hardest working nobody in the business'.

How do you practically look to the future when things are changing so rapidly?

The way I do it is to look at what I call *the fringe*.

Which is?

Basically, the fringe is three deviations away from the mean! If we want to see the parts of the future that are seeable we need to look at the fringe because the fringe migrates to the middle.

So, trends that are peripheral become mainstream?

Exactly. The book I'm now working on – something called *Abso-**&!!-lutely*, complete with ampersands and exclamation marks – is a deconstruction of the fringe. It's Studs Terkel territory. Lots of stories. It is about more than recognizing that the fringe is different. The fringe isn't what it used to be or where it used to be. The fringe is now found in different places. It's migratory, transitory.

So you've become a cool hunter, someone who seeks out the latest trend in the inner city and takes it to the mass market?

On the contrary. Most people looking at the fringe are looking at what is mainstream. Cool hunters look in the wrong places. By the time cool hunters say this is the edge, it's already moved significantly to the mainstream. The fringe is moving so quickly. It's whether you find yourself in the story that's important. You have to make up the fringe for yourself.

Given all this, how do you connect with reality?

Reality may have become an artefact. We are increasingly devoid of context. Going to museums is the greatest out-of-house activity in the world. A good futurist is usually a better historian. Too many futurists are perceived as naïve optimists. Mark Twain said that history doesn't repeat itself but it sure does rhyme. You have to acknowledge how you got where you are.

I'm intrigued by different types of museum. I like Churchill's war rooms and traditional museums, but also there's something like five museums to the Unabomber. What I love about the US is that we're the only country that builds monuments to its failures – Custer's last stand has a museum; there's a memorial at Pearl Harbour.

Going to museums is the cornerstone of learning about different cultures. One of the first things I always do when I visit somewhere is to see what the new museums are.

Another subject close to your heart is branding. What makes for a great brand?

Great brands tend to be referred to by their customers and even their competitors as being genuine and authentic. Whenever authenticity is associated with a brand, the brand tends to have reached a level of involvement in its consuming universe that is of mythological proportions. Anything that causes a 'disconnect' between that authenticity and the actions taken by the brand will result in an immediate and severe consumer response. For example, Lite beer was built for 35-year-old ex-jocks. As the brand's marketplace began to reach saturation, Miller's response to the desire for continued growth was to 'contemporize' the brand and go after a younger market. Suddenly, the 35-year-old ex-jocks felt like this beer no longer fits them. And the younger group never felt like it was designed for them in the first place.

You talk of 'cohort brands' and 'life stage brands'. Can you explain the difference?

Cohort brands are those that become attached to a group of people and travel over time with them. Life stage brands are used at specific stages of life. For example, mothers use Coppertone on their young children and then slather themselves with the same product. The children themselves grow into the next life stage brand (like Hawaiian Tropic and Tropical Blend), then grow into another life stage and use Bain de Soleil. When they get married and have kids, they come back to using Coppertone.

The importance of understanding life stage versus cohort is also reflected in the ups and downs of Nike. Whether this was to do with the brand itself or athletic shoes in general, at a certain point the target audience for Nike sneakers (teens and young adults) no longer wanted to wear a shoe that was so ubiquitous their parents were wearing the same brand.

How involved in the branding should a chief executive get?

The chief executive's biggest job is to be the ombudsman for the brand. The most important asset in any firm is its brand. Everything else is replaceable. The chief executive is the custodian of that brand's reputation. All decisions should be made to be consistent with the brand's three circumstances: its history, its vision for its future, and the circumstances that it finds itself in at any moment. This is more difficult than it appears to be.

What else should they do?

Good chief executives have to be the counter intuitive force of the firm as well. Most people only hire people like themselves. CEOs must recognize that they need to hire people that are not like themselves. Harry Truman once said, 'I don't have to be the smartest son-of-a-bitch in the world, I just have to have them working for me'. I think Harry was right.

Is the future going to bring new organizational forms – such as business clubs?

The future is OK; most people just don't know it yet. 'Access' is a given today (demand-based versus supply-based world); nothing is more available than money – though it's sitting on the sideline temporarily – and the world GDP is on its way to $40 trillion. Business clubs and businesses trying to act like clubs are 'hawking' access to ideas, not networks or money or prestige or even self-esteem. My concern is that they all end up simply talking to themselves – 80% of McKinsey's clients are ex-McKinsey people.

Networks need to be created and disbanded on a case-by-case need. The network for this deal may be useless for the next. To date, clubs are too static for a world driven by situational ethics and values. A project team is a club while the project exists (including its own logos).

I'm still convinced that being unknown will become the biggest status symbol in an age of (over)celebrity so I do not agree with the 'identity' issue … unless it's for people who are followers('fast' or not).

As to communities of like interests, to have community one must have sacrifice. Community only happens when an individual is willing to make a sacrifice to be a part of something bigger than themselves, which THEY choose to be a part of. Where are the sacrifices?

I do think 'clubs' will grow because business is scared shitless about what to do.

JOHN PATRICK: THE ATTITUDE THING

John Patrick is a founding member and chairman of the Global Internet Project and a founding member of the World Wide Web Consortium at MIT. He is best known for leading IBM's charge into the new world of e-business. After 35 years with IBM, where he was Chief Internet Technology Officer, Patrick is now a speaker and author. His first book is Net Attitude.

How would you describe yourself?

I am not a consultant; that's not my thing. I like to write and speak and participate on boards so I would describe myself as an author, lecturer and hobbyist. I love technology. I like acquiring it. Look at this digital camera I have just bought. It's Japanese – called 'Che-ez!' – you wear it around your neck, it's very small and has a USB connection. So I like to fool with technology.

The thing I'm into at the moment is blogging; building and maintaining a Web log. It is similar to discussion groups but the best description is that a Web log is a diary. I have just written one about a spray paint I bought! People are now making a living from blogging and I think that blogging may well emerge as potentially the primary source of published material. That's radical but possible.

So, I enjoy communicating, sharing experiences and over the years I've learned to communicate fairly well I think.

Are you a computer nerd?

I don't think of myself as a nerd. I've been a CFO and involved in business management.

Some people have a passion for golf, I don't – I would just as soon be doing something with my computer. I don't consider emails as work. It is communicating with people so I don't measure how much time I spend answering emails.

The thing I don't enjoy is spam. It is now encroaching on our personal lives in a very offensive way. People are stealing our time and I'm very concerned about this.

I hope that the only answer isn't government regulation. I'm hoping for creative, technical ways to deal with this. The solution, I think, is authentication. Authentication means having a digital ID so if someone without an ID sends you an email, the message will be automatically deleted. If the sender has an ID you still need to know who gave them the ID and then you might read the message. Authentication solves a lot of problems. Authentication is the empowerment which will enable e-commerce to go onto the next step and help eliminate spam.

So you don't like the anonymity offered by email?

The important thing is that if I can establish that you are who you say you are, I can establish the level of privacy I want. Anonymity is okay. I don't think most people want to be anonymous, but think of battered wives, for example, who might want and need to be anonymous.

What about issues of privacy?

People feel that the government is going to track them but people should feel empowered. Authentication would give you confidentiality. Now, most emails aren't encrypted so they can be read. If you had a private key only you can then read your emails. These things are technically available but it is a leadership issue. It is time for leaders of governments, financial organizations, educational institutions and other bodies to step forward and take a leadership role. In Spain, digital IDs have been distributed to people so they can look at their taxes online.

Isn't part of the problem that the Internet is beyond the control of a single body or government?

The magic of the Internet is that no one individual or body is in charge. Instead, there are lots of working groups and standards groups without which there wouldn't be an Internet.

There is no central plank on which the Internet relies and without which it would fall apart. There have been predictions of the Internet's collapse over the years but it is highly distributed. September

11 destroyed important portions of the Internet but it carried on. Just think that ten years ago people were saying that the Internet was not scaleable and that it was insecure and unstable.

Yes, ten years ago the Internet was viewed with some scepticism, even by technology companies.

Most people, and companies like Microsoft and IBM as well as many others, viewed the Internet as interesting but little more.

The grassroots proved otherwise. The grassroots is made up of a lot of smart people throughout the world who have a passion for technology and solving problems. Problems will be solved by working groups made up of volunteers.

At the moment the Internet is not as reliable as the telephone system but which would you rather have?

How did IBM come to the Internet so early in its development?

When Lou Gerstner came along and saw the Internet he saw its potential. He is a great communicator and he saw its power. At that time, e-business hadn't been invented so he didn't know where the business opportunity lay but knew that it was a powerful communication mechanism.

Gary Hamel has celebrated your role in Internet development at IBM.

I was trying to get the grassroots together, then I went outside IBM and talked to people and got a lot of press coverage. Gary may have given me more credit than I deserved. There were a lot of heroes at IBM.

Weren't you ever tempted to leave IBM?

I had a constant barrage from headhunters to go to California and run this and that company. But the best opportunity lay at IBM because it has great people and great resources – around 3000 PhDs involved in research.

The Internet galvanized the company. There had been a time when the company had no strategy then e-business became the strategy. Everyone suddenly knew that that was our business.

You were in the right place at the right time.

At a personal level, there was a certain amount of luck and serendipity in all this. I've been involved in a few fortunate things. The thing with IBM and the Internet is that lots of people have great ideas but can't communicate them very well. Lou Gerstner sent out a booklet entitled 'One Voice' in 1995 or 1996 to the home addresses of everyone in the company. It said that the Internet was our future. He encouraged people to try things, to use the Internet. Our worry was that people weren't using the Internet enough. We weren't bothered about people looking at pornographic sites – one employee who did was fired – our bigger concern was getting people oriented around the Internet.

How did you get older managers involved?

One of the things IBM does is reverse mentoring. A 25-year-old is assigned to a senior vice president.

Now, of course, people over 65 are one of the fastest growing sectors of Internet use. They have grandchildren who won't write or call but who will send email.

How can you maximize your e-business?

All the technology and money on the planet won't enable you to meet people's expectations if you don't have the right attitude.

What is the right attitude?

It is an attitude that includes the ability to think globally but act locally, think big but start simple, think outside-in instead of inside-out, be able to accept 'just enough is good enough', engage in trial by fire, transform to a model of sense and respond instead of the traditional model of plan, build, deliver. This attitude comes from the grassroots thinking that was part of the evolution of the Internet. It's hard to describe. Young people tend to have it but it's not really an age thing. The masses of people in the middle layers of large organizations often don't have it. The bureaucracies of large organizations have shielded them from the new way of thinking and, in some cases, Darwinian instincts have caused them to bring up their own shields.

What's the next big thing?

One thing which is emerging in the US is WiFi, wireless fidelity, which will become a huge thing. It reminds me of the Internet ten years ago.

The last mile is getting high speed connections into the home. Now you don't need to involve the phone or cable company, you can do it through wireless. Community-based wireless access is emerging. I can feel the grassroots nature of what's taking off. People are making antennae from a Pringles can and putting it on the roof of their buildings. These things have a range of a few miles and mean that people can use the broadband technology used by their employers when they're at home.

I was in a sandwich shop in a small town in Connecticut and wondered if there were any wireless networks in the air. There were and I was soon connected at 1.3 million bits per second. I don't know where the signal was coming from but I was connected and didn't have to pay.

When CIOs hear this they shudder. They say it's insecure, unreliable, etc. – the same list as ten years ago when they talked about the Internet.

Soon people are going to expect to be able to be connected. Think of all the places where people wait – at the doctors, the dentists, coffee shops. All the issues are soluble.

We are on the verge of a new era for the Internet that's as big and exciting as the first. It will have seven characteristics – fast, always on, everywhere, natural, intelligent, easy and trusted. The pace is accelerating with more competition, fewer barriers to entry and high expectations. At the moment we are only 5 per cent into the Internet's ability.

So the mobile workforce is a reality.

Yes, the mobile workforce is a reality. In fact I think it has been for quite some time. It is one of those things that just creeps up on society; no arrival date, no cutover date, etc. It has been happening for ten years. Initially it was the heat seekers, then the early adopters, and now it is moving into the majority. I would say that most people in business today telecommute somewhat. It is a bell curve. The fact that it is hard to measure precisely is precisely the point. To telecommute used to be a big deal; you had to know a lot, have a lot of special equipment, etc. to make it feasible. Now anyone can do it.

With 802.11, WiFi, this is going to accelerate. People will be online doing work while they are at the airport, coffee shop, or in the waiting room of a hospital or doctors office.

If technology is so good why is service so bad?

Technology has definitely increased the ability for e-businesses to offer world-class customer service but unfortunately, I believe that the gap between what people expect and what they get is growing. People expect to be able to make an online hotel reservation and pay for it with their choice of airline frequent flier miles or track the progress of something they ordered through the entire supply chain and be able to return it to a physical store. Yes, there are some great Web sites out there but there are also many that have taken their old processes and attitudes and moved them to the Web. Click here for more information and you often get 'stop in and see one of our agents 9–5 M–F', or 'fill out this form and fax it to us so we can send you an owner's manual', 'your order has been processed, if you want to check the status of it, give us a call', and so on. Organizations of all kinds have to think about what it means to be 'open'. The words 9–5 M–F mean nothing to teenagers and yet they soon will be an even bigger force in the marketplace – as employees and consumers – than they already are. Call centres are another example of the need to change. People are quite tired of hearing 'please pay attention because our menus have changed'. How could it be that all menus in the world have recently changed? The bottom line is integration. Organizations need to integrate their islands of automation so that they can meet the rapidly rising expectations of their customers.

CHARLES HANDY: REFLECTIONS OF A RELUCTANT CAPITALIST

No other management theorist's world view encompasses the irresistible rise of the flea, the crumbling of the elephants and a written constitution for business. In addition, the world according to Charles Handy calls on the business world to rethink the money-obsessed mindset of executives and to look for a reason for business beyond simply increasing shareholder value.

Charles Handy, the UK's only home-grown international management guru, has long been regarded as one of the most eminent and influential business thinkers in the world.

Irish-born Handy is a former oil executive turned academic and is now enjoying a third career as a populist social philosopher. For reading the business runes or stretching the imagination, he has few equals. Yet, despite his often revolutionary message, his remains the genteel, civilized voice of management.

Handy worked for Shell until 1972 when he left to teach at London Business School where he was the first director of LBS's Sloan Management Programme. Since then he has written a number of bestselling books including Understanding Organisations (1976), The Age of Unreason (1989), The Hungry Spirit (1998), and, most recently, The Elephant and the Flea (2002).

Among his best known ideas is that of the 'cloverleaf organization' – later called the shamrock organization – with a small core at the centre of a system of 'leaves' made up of outsourced work, contractors, consultants and temporary workers. Revolutionary at the time, it turned out to be an accurate prediction of the future.

Handy has been challenging the status quo ever since. To him, capitalism is a system – the best we've come up with so far – but merely a beginning. It is a stepping-off point for what really matters to human beings – their aspirations, families and sense of self-worth. His 1998 book The Hungry Spirit warned of the dangers of the mercenary society that corporations had created.

So how does Handy view today's turbulent business environment?

You use a lot of metaphors in your work. How helpful are they to practising managers?

I think they're very helpful to understanding things. When they're in a hurry people think better visually than they do analytically.

My metaphors are basically visual – the elephant and the flea, for example. Now that doesn't tell you what to do but it does jerk you and make you look at your organization and yourself in a different way and I think that's the first step to practicality, to understanding where you are and what the possibilities are. Then you have to work out what exactly you do. I don't go that next step in my writing. I don't tell people what to do. I think that though there are generalities every individual situation is just a little bit different. So though I would give examples I wouldn't be specific. I like to leave it at the metaphor level.

It's a user-friendly way of getting into quite serious issues. It's a lot easier than talking about things like re-engineering – where you have to find out what it means because it doesn't immediately tell you anything. Metaphors immediately tell you something.

So your metaphors deliberately go in the opposite direction to the mechanistic language of a lot of management ideas?

Absolutely. I talk about doughnuts and shamrocks and all that sort of stuff. First of all it intrigues people. Second, as I said, it is user-friendly. And, third, it is terribly useful. My shamrock model, for example, is a way of describing how organizations are carving themselves up into sub-contractors and so on. I went to a conference in the US about ten years ago, soon after that book came out there, and I met a group of people who told me they worked for the Shamrock Organization. I said how funny and they said no, we call it that because we read your book and decided to practice exactly what you said; so we decided to call ourselves the Shamrock Organization.

Is there a new model that you see developing now?

Well for the elephants, the big organizations, there is what I call the federal model. It's another metaphor – not quite as homespun as shamrock and drawn from political theory – which is becoming increasingly significant. We are now realizing that organizations are not mechanistic devices but communities of people. Therefore political theory – winning acceptance for your ideas, talking about leadership rather than management are all political ideas – is becoming relevant. It is about how you get communities to move in a certain direction. Federalism is a political idea that we know quite a lot about and which I believe is terribly relevant to large global organizations where some things have to be centralized and others must be decentralized.

For example, federalism says that you have to have a common law and a common currency. So, translating that into organization terms there have to be some basic rules. Some of these big organizations have a 'bible' – a set of basic principles or rules for how we behave. And they have a common currency, by which I mean a common information system.

In the UK we don't have a written constitution as they do in the US. Do companies need a written constitution?

I think they do. Federalism is all about negotiation as to who does what and who has the power and authority for what. It's not hierarchical. In a mechanistic model it's easy for an organization to say the top man does everything and the bottom man has limits to his authority; the top man can tell the second top man what to do and everyone knows where the authority is down the line. But it's much more complicated in a federal organization. A federal organization is often made up of alliances and partnerships and you actually do have to negotiate who has the power to do what and it really does need to be written down. These are legally binding things because you're dealing with partners who may have a share of the operation. So a constitution has to be written down.

And the 'constitution' becomes a higher authority that people can appeal to?

That's right. There is a sort of 'supreme court' function that is usually a sub-committee of the board – the audit committee or the oversight committee. The other interesting thing about the federal model is that there is a legislative function and an executive function – and they are different, though they may overlap to some degree. The executive function proposes things to the legislative function, which lays down the law. I think that's increasingly happening in organizations.

You no longer have dictatorships at the top. Call it corporate governance or whatever, but the chief executive increasingly does not have total power to set the rules, to set the laws. It has to be done by a representative body and increasingly that body has to represent other interests than just the shareholders. People talk about the community and so on but I also think it has to represent employees and other members of the alliance, who then entitle and enable the

CEO to do what he or she has to do. The CEO has to be obedient to these groups.

One big difference with a political leader, for example the US president, is that he is the elected representative of the people. Can you see companies electing CEOs in the future?

I don't think it's impossible. I think the electorate would be confined to people who are directly in touch with him or her. I can't see Coca-Cola polling everyone to elect a president. It wouldn't be feasible. But I can see a more informal process going on, where soundings are taken – rather like the Conservative party of old in the UK. When boards have to change CEOs they do canvas opinion – but usually not enough within the organization; they canvas outside. But increasingly I think they will canvas inside. Because to exercise authority in the modern organization it's not enough to have the position; you have to have the acceptance of your authority – your right to rule – to get people to do anything.

Would a written constitution have prevented what happened at Enron?

No. I don't think so because there was an informal constitution there that would have overridden it. They overrode it with the permission of the supreme court function in the form of the auditing body and the board, which theoretically knew what was going on. So even if they'd had a written constitution they would have been able to override it. I suppose it might have helped to concentrate minds.

This is going to happen. Increasingly, non-executive directors and trustees of charities are beginning to realize that they are liable and that they will have to pay more attention to what's going on. And I think they will want what *should* be going on to be written down. So I think written constitutions will be coming in.

Another strand in your more recent work has been the role of the entrepreneur. Are we at a point where everyone now has to see himself or herself as an entrepreneur?

No. Though we are all responsible for our own lives to a greater extent than we were, that doesn't mean we will all be entrepreneurs although we all need to think of ourselves much more as independent agents. OK, we may be currently working for, employed by, or indentured to a corporation but that's not a guarantee anymore. When organizations decide to get rid of 30,000 people, a lot of those people are going to be very surprised. They may get a good pay-off but they have to realize that that particular stage of their life may have come to an end and nobody is going to look after them in the way they used to. In that sense we are all independent agents.

Now, the degree to which we're entrepreneurs is another question. We're not all going to be setting up independent businesses.

Entrepreneurs in the sense of being entrepreneurial units of one?

Yes. 'Me Inc.' I think so more and more. I think we will increasingly see a career with an organization as an apprenticeship – rather like going to college before you set out on your own – and I think that's a very good thing. We would be very rash to think we could set up on our own without going to college and without any experience of the business world. That apprenticeship may go on for 20 years but even that brings you only to your early or mid-40s.

I think increasingly most of the elephants are going to have a managerial core with an average age of around the mid-30s, with a few wise old owls who stay, but an awful lot of people peeling off at around 40 and setting up on their own or in partnership and selling their services back into the elephants.

The elephants will be organizers rather than doing everything. And the people they organize may well be ex-employees who have been spun off to do their own thing. Maybe the corporation will keep a stake in them so it has it both ways. So organizations that see themselves as the seedbeds of future independent business people will be doing themselves and everyone else a big favour.

That's a very different career path for an individual. So how does someone acquire a mindset that says they're going to join an organization from college and then make that major adjustment in their late 30s?

At the moment it's probably in their late 40s but the age when people become fleas of one kind or another will come down. I think you have to change the *zeitgeist* – to say to people the world has changed. That's why I use metaphors to try to popularize the idea that there are elephants that are very big and visible but that in fact most people don't actually work for them. Most people work for fleas – small organizations – or are themselves fleas.

I went out to dinner the other day with a family we know and the father took me on one side and said I've just been made redundant and I'm going to set up as a consultant with a friend – what do you think of that? And I said, well, you've become a flea. And then I talked to his daughter, who's an investment banker, and she said I've just taken voluntary redundancy in the City and I'm going to be an independent person and I'm not going to do banking again. I sold my whole life to this great bank in Canary Wharf and I'm not going to do it anymore.

So here were two people I thought were good respectable elephant people who totally unexpectedly – and I see them about once a month – were telling me that they had become fleas. They weren't frightened; they were looking forward to it. They've served their apprenticeships; they know they have talents and they've got some money because they've been well paid. As more and more of that happens – and, indeed, the concept of the flea is legitimized – I think you'll hear more people talking about being fleas.

Redundancy has lost much of its stigma?

Yes. The other term I coined a few years ago was portfolio career – portfolio jobs and portfolio workers – and that seems to have become accepted as a respectable thing to be.

You have some concerns about portfolio careers, though?

Well not everyone can cope with it. When I did it I discovered two things. The first was that I had some skills that I didn't realize were saleable – namely writing and speaking – which were nothing to do with my first career as an oil executive. Second, I discovered someone to sell them – my wife, who turned out to be a brilliant agent and businesswoman. It doesn't have to be your life partner but you need somebody to help you. Indeed, to do everything on your own is very lonely. And even if you employ people it's still very lonely. You need a partner, I think, to help you think things through and to compensate for the skills you don't have, which in my case are marketing and being a good businessman.

But lots of people don't do that. I get people writing to me saying they've accepted voluntary redundancy and are going portfolio. They've read my books and ask me to please help them fill their portfolios. And I say I can't do that. You've got to discover your skills and market yourself. I tell them it will take two years to build the kind of brand recognition that they need and they'll have to work very, very hard.

How do you build that kind of brand recognition?

It basically comes from doing good work in the first place – and a certain word of mouth. But you can help the word of mouth by giving yourself some kind of image. Putting a word or something on that image – so you get known for something. It's no good just saying I'm a strategy consultant because there are a lot of strategy consultants around. So what's your particular take on life? Maybe it's the process by which you go about it – or maybe the ideas you have or the particular marketplace you operate in – 'he's the sort of guy that does this sort of thing'. So you've got to find a way of encapsulating that. And then you promote the brand basically by word of mouth though you can also write articles, give speeches and all that sort of thing. But it takes time. You can try hiring a PR agent but I don't think that really works.

Do your ideas work equally well in developing countries such as India or China?

It does vary with the culture. Italy, for example, is a country of small businesses so it is naturally a flea land. Being a flea is totally accepted. But not so much in Spain, which is a hierarchical organization place – people like to feel they belong to an organization

I think India is a land of fleas although maybe they are still at the stage where they need to grow a few more elephants. Because I'm not saying that elephants are doomed. Fleas need elephants because they are the organizers. Without them fleas would have nothing to crawl on and feed on. We need elephants. I don't know China well enough to really comment. But again it seems to me it may need to grow some more elephants.

I think the concepts do apply but perhaps there are different stages in the mix of elephants and fleas. And the relationship between them is very important. If you treat fleas just as suppliers and you make them go out to tender and push down their costs then you won't get the best out of them. You've got to treat them more as the Japanese would in their *keiretsu*. I once read that Toyota had 30,000 suppliers – those are mostly fleas selling into this huge elephant. If you look closely, all countries are like that – a small number of big elephants with lots of fleas clustering around them. People just haven't looked at it in that way. They talk about SMEs – small and medium-sized enterprises – which is frightfully boring. It's a technical description but doesn't give you any sense of the dynamism and flexibility of the flea culture that I think is so important.

You have been critical of the mercenary culture that exists among managers in big business. What causes it and how does it impact on society?

Yes, I'm concerned that capitalism is eating itself. I think money is an essential ingredient in successful societies. Most families that break down do so because the economics go wrong rather than the love disappears. I never want to be heard to say that money is not important. But it is a means to another end.

I think the danger with capitalism and with organizations and businesses is that money has become the end. We are just competing for who can get the most money – whether it's a corporation, an industry or an entrepreneur. I find that deadening to the human spirit. You can never win that race. You may be Bill Gates for a time but sure as hell there'll be another Bill Gates and so unless you start to use your money for another purpose – as, to be fair, Bill Gates seems to be doing – it is meaningless.

Of course if you are successful in business you will make money. But then you can only go on being a successful business if you continue to do something that is more useful to more people than other businesses and you need money to grow to do that. So I think the purpose of business is not to make money but to do something that is more useful to more people than anybody else. But most capitalists don't think about it that way, I'm afraid.

And most managers don't think about it that way, either. They want promotion because they can make more money to pay off a bigger mortgage and have a bigger house rather than because they can now be in a position to do something more worthy with their lives.

In The Elephant and the Flea there's a passage about your father's funeral and how it made you re-evaluate the meaning of success. Do you think managers have lost a sense of how to define success beyond just money?

For too many people that's true. Money is an easy thing to count. It's easy to put a scale on it and say someone is more successful than someone else. I think many people discover too late in their lives that that isn't it. Success is something else. Luckily I discovered it in the middle of my life rather than at the end.

Does fleadom offer a second chance?

When I was working for an oil company my goals were quite clear:

to get more responsibility. I'd already sold my time to them for the next 40 years so the only question was what was I going to do with that time. And they would tell me that. The only question, therefore, that I could negotiate was how much they were going to pay me for my time. So obviously I was interested in more money, almost to the exclusion of anything else.

But when I became an independent flea I realized that there was a trade-off. I could sell all my waking hours and make quite a lot of money. But on the other hand, I didn't have to do that. I could sell half my time and make half as much money. So then you have to say to yourself what do I really want to do with my life? That's why I say in the end it's a question of philosophy not of economics. You do have to say: what is my life about; how do I count success; how do I want to be remembered; what difference do I want to make in the world – oh and by the way, I need some money. But how much money and what am I going to sacrifice if I want more money?

My wife and I set strict limits on how much money because it takes up a lot of time. We try to do only things that we think are really useful; a bit of prostitution to pay for the groceries.

'Looking back to the future' *is the subtitle of* **The Elephant and the Flea. Why did you choose that?**

Well it was too clever really. It was meant to say that I was looking back at my life and drawing lessons for the future – not for me particularly but for other people. So the book is an autobiography of these reflections. The US edition has a different subtitle – *Reflections of a reluctant capitalist*. I quite like that because it describes the book and me quite well. I am a slightly sceptical reluctant capitalist. I don't know of anything better but I'm not totally convinced it's doing everything well at the moment. And it is a book of reflections not prescriptions.

Do you think the anti-capitalist protests are a significant movement or somewhat marginal?

At the moment it's at the margin but it's expressing a feeling that many of the younger generation, and some of the older, feel – that the elephants are getting too powerful. I'm not so worried about it because I don't think they can tell governments what to do. But there is that worry. Then there's the deeper concern that capitalism is eroding our values – what we've just been talking about

– that materialism is dominating everything else and that money is the measure of all things. Third, that the world is growing more unequal, particularly internationally, and many countries are not getting any better.

I share all those concerns. I don't share their methodology. They have to attract attention. If you have peaceful protests no one notices. At the moment it's at the margin but I think they are reflecting a growing unease, which I share, about where we are heading with this. And I don't have any easy answers – nor do they. The problem is they are protesting but they don't have any answers.

The only answers, I think, lie with changing the mindsets of the people who run these organizations. And I think that is changing. They're beginning to see that they need to be less preoccupied with themselves and more with their bigger purpose in life. That's not the same as social responsibility – which is a phrase I don't like. I just want them to define their aims in a more helpful, unselfish way. We have to find better ways to make that legitimate, so that CEOs can go and stand before their financiers – their shareholders – and say this is what we're doing and it is acceptable.

Social responsibility isn't the right way because it looks like just having good PR. It has to be something bigger than that. I don't have the words yet. I suppose it ought to be my next book.

'Proper selfishness' is another term you've used. It seems like an individual quality rather than an organizational one. Can you explain?

Yes it is, though in *The Hungry Spirit* I tried to apply it to organizations as well. You've first of all got to look after yourself. If as an individual you're not at ease with yourself then you're no good to anyone else. The same applies to corporations. If they are not healthy and thriving they are no good to anyone else.

Having done that, to make it proper selfishness you have to use that selfishness for some greater purpose beyond yourself. That is the bit that's lacking. The selfishness bit is there. There are a lot of very fit individuals and very fit corporations around the place but what are they going to do? It's what I've been calling recently the second level of success. The first level of success is proving that you are OK; the second level of success is then doing something with that.

There are some – usually small individually owned corporations or family firms – with a mission to do something other than just to make money. When they've got lots of money they say they want to make the best wine in the world or something.

My other thesis is that the balance of power has got to shift a bit away from shareholders, who finance the wealth creation, to the people who actually make the wealth. I think that's going to happen not because I say so but because we've got to find better ways to reward the people who make the wealth – that probably means giving them an increasing share of the equity. Some of it will happen through putting shares in the company into trusts for the workers and so on. Share options are a rather insidious way of making cost-free payments to people. But I do think that if you or your group are responsible for making the wealth then you should have as much of a stake in the future of the corporation as the people who finance it. The idea of ownership will gradually go. The financiers will become less powerful and the employees will become voters as it were. That would be healthy.

But even if you're a business leader it's very hard to change the system. You are going to be judged on your financial performance.

What I worry about with capitalism is that so much of it is just trading businesses – buying and selling. These businesses are communities of people; they are like villages or towns. It's like buying York and selling it to Spain. I really don't think it's very nice. But under the present systems of Anglo-American open stock markets capitalism, it's very difficult to see how you can stop that. The only way I think it's going to change is to change the culture – that means CEOs standing up and saying, 'I'm not going for maximizing shareholder value in the short-term, I'm building a great community with enough vitality to last 50 years'.

Now the mission may change over time but we're not just going to buy any bloody company just so we can look at our balance sheet growing and growing. We are a supermarket. We are there to offer people wonderful produce. But when they all start becoming banks as well as everything else you really start to wonder who's going to manage these strange organizations.

Is there a point at which someone can recognize that they are ready to embrace their fleadom?

I think people know. When the fun goes out of the job and you see people passing you by. But by that time you may be starting to lose your confidence too. I have a diagram in one of my books of two curves and you have to start the second curve before the first one peaks so you have time to build it up. So it's getting the first signs of that peaking and it probably comes not from being bored but from complacency. When you think you know it all. I left academic life when I fell asleep in one of my own lectures – because it was just so easy. I knew that I'd stopped growing. Very soon that starts to become boredom.

But you're not bored with writing books yet?

Well I'm beginning to be bored of writing these sorts of books. So I'm going to change. I'm going to work more with my wife on interesting people – a mixture of text and photographs. We're thinking of doing one called *Double Harness* about people like us who work together, where one of the partners runs the back office and the other runs the front. How they set their priorities and manage their relationships. Not just glamorous people – but electricians and plumbers and priests and doctors whose wives often do the books and manage the financial side. We haven't paid enough attention to back office roles but they are probably really important.

But I probably won't write any more books about the big world of corporates because I feel I've said everything I have to say about it. I'd just be repeating myself.

PHILIP KOTLER: MARKETING IN THE DIGITAL AGE

Now in his seventies, Philip Kotler remains prolific. The world's pre-eminent marketing thinker has over 25 books to his name, including Marketing Moves *(written with Dipak Jain and Suvit Maesincee).*

Kotler started out as an economist and studied under Nobel Prize winners Milton Friedman and Paul Samuelson. He then became fascinated by marketing. Seeking out textbooks on the subject he was disappointed to find them heavily descriptive rather than helpfully prescriptive. So, he wrote Marketing Management, *still the definitive work on marketing and the textbook on every marketing student's shelves.*

Subsequently, Kotler has applied marketing theory to a huge variety of new areas – nonprofit organizations (museums, performing arts, hospitals, colleges, etc.), social causes, places (cities, regions, and nations), and celebrities. Along the way he has coined phrases such as 'mega marketing', 'demarketing', 'social marketing', 'place marketing', and 'segmentation, targeting, and positioning'.

Kotler, a professor at Northwestern University, has a flair for neat and useful definitions. 'When I am asked to define marketing in the briefest possible way, I say marketing is meeting needs profitably. A lot of us meet needs – but businesses are set up to do it profitably', he says. 'Marketing is the homework that you do to hit the mark that satisfies those needs exactly. When you do that job, there isn't much selling work to do because the word gets out from delighted customers that this is a wonderful solution to our problems.'

In this interview, Kotler surveys the new world of online marketing and offers his insights on marketing in the digital age.

Why has marketing been slow to respond to changes in markets?

Markets always change faster than marketing. Companies have ingrained practices and fairly frozen allocations of marketing funds. Each function – advertising, sales promotion, sales force – wants the same or a large budget each year independent of whether the function is gaining or losing productivity. It doesn't matter whether advertising is losing its effectiveness. This is why marketing practice remains out-of-touch with the new marketplace.

What is a holistic approach to marketing?

Marketing has too often been treated as a department, one that essentially carries out marketing communications and promotions. In *Marketing Moves*, we argue that marketing, properly conceived, is a strategic function and should be the driver of company strategy. Peter Drucker noted this with his famous questions put to companies: 'What business are you in? Who are your customers? What is value to the customers?' He went on to say: 'The two most important functions of a company are marketing and innovation.' Our holistic approach develops this further and calls for marketing to be the architect of the company's demand and supply chain and its network of collaborators.

What effect has the advent of the new economy and the Internet had on your thinking and on marketing?

I became fascinated with the implications of e-commerce and e-business for business strategy. At first I thought that pure click operators such as Amazon and Yahoo! would have a tremendous competitive advantage, as they owned few physical assets. My mind changed when I saw how much they had to spend on marketing to build their brand and attract and keep customers.

I believe that the Internet will fundamentally change business and marketing practice. I expect that the price transparency of the Internet will put great pressure on prices. I expect the emergence of business-to-business Web sites will reduce the number of salespeople involved in routine sales work. I expect to see companies increasingly differentiate their services to different tiers of customers according to customer lifetime value.

Where do the main online opportunities lie for marketers?

Some companies illustrate the power of online commerce when it is done well. Dell Computer has exploited the Internet as way to help customers customize their computers and transact at a lower cost to both the customers and Dell. Amazon offers not only the largest number of available books online but value-added information in the form of editorial and customer reviews. Not everything can be sold online profitably, as many dot-coms have found out. The truth is that the importance of the Internet far exceeds its use as an e-commerce tool.

You call on managers to completely redefine their companies. But isn't the managerial ability and enthusiasm to do this extremely limited?

> The scarce resource is creativity, not managerial ability or enthusiasm. Companies can only thrive in a hypercompetitive market by continually improving and inventing. Yet so few companies put a premium on new ideas or manage any system to capture them.

What is the difference between marketplace and marketspace?

> If I go to a Barnes and Noble bookstore to buy a book, I am transacting in the marketplace. If I go on www.barnesandnoble.com, I am transacting in marketspace (called cyberspace).

Haven't successful companies always realized that the customer is king?

> Although the customer is king today, this is not always the case. He is not king in the face of a monopolist. Nor is he king during periods of shortage. Much depends on whether there is a shortage of goods or customers. When customers are scarce, businesses will have to compete for them and cater to them. That's today's situation.

You talk of there being four customer wants – change, participation, freedom and stability. Is this a new concept?

> No. This serves only as a useful framework for analyzing markets and identifying market segments. People differ in the weights they put on change, participation, freedom and stability and these weights change over time and circumstance.

Are the four Ps of marketing still relevant or useful?

> The four Ps of marketing – product, price, place, and promotion – serve as useful building blocks for constructing the marketing mix to carry out the firm's strategy to win a chosen target market. Each P carries a subset of tools for influencing the level, timing, and composition of demand. Thus, there is a product mix, price mix, place mix, and promotion mix that must be established in preparing the marketing battle plans.

How can companies capitalize on the emergence of metamarkets?

A metamarket facilitates all of the activities involved in obtaining an item for use or consumption. To buy a car, I must choose the car, finance it and get insurance. Thus, Edmunds.com represents an online metamarket where I will get information about all cars, search for the best dealer for the car I want, arrange for a loan, and buy insurance. Knots.com represents an online metamarket for obtaining everything connected with preparing a wedding, including gowns, invitation cards, gifts, and the like.

Is it still useful to talk of old and new economies?

Today's economy is a hybrid of an industrial economy (where manufacturing predominates) and a post-industrial economy (marked more by services, finance, globalization and technology). At best, we can describe today's economy as a hybrid economy with old and new elements.

Is global marketing becoming more adaptive to the growing markets of Asia and India?

Many anticipate that this century will be called the Asian century. Japan made a strong beginning in the 1970s followed by the five smaller dragons of South Korea, Thailand, Malaysia, Singapore, and Hong Kong. They all hit a wall in the late 1990s but will come back. China now is showing the most exuberance, growing as one of the world's leading manufacturing powers. India is less organized but represents huge market potential for investors.

Can and should the United States be marketed? And, if so, how?

The US is marketed everywhere everyday, for good or bad, by McDonald's, Coca-Cola, and Hollywood. It advertises its brand of capitalism as one of free markets, free trade, and freedom of the press. It attracts admiration, it attracts envy, and it attracts censure for many of its ways and outcomes. I think that the US needs a fresh marketing programme that drops some of the old rhetoric and presents a new view of universal values and aspirations, not limited to the seeming cowboy mentality that its leaders project.

What is the best marketing job in the world?

> The most satisfying marketing job is not to sell more Coca-Cola or Crest toothpaste but to bring more education and health to people and make a real difference in the quality of their lives.

Section 3
PEOPLE POWER

For the past 200 years, the dominant metaphor of business has been the machine. The men who led the transformation to an industrial economy were engineers and factory owners. To them, the company was an extension of the means by which mass production was made possible. The company itself was best understood as an engine of wealth.

Mechanistic metaphors still hold sway in many areas of business. The big management idea of the mid-1990s, for example, was re-engineering. In the name of re-engineering, companies were taken apart like so many car engines and reassembled by efficiency enthusiasts. In the company as machine, people are no more than cogs. Even now managers talk about workers being re-tooled rather than retrained.

Today, however, the mechanistic metaphor is increasingly being challenged. There is a move towards the notion of the company as a living system. It is an idea championed by thinkers such as former Royal Dutch/Shell executive Arie de Geus. His highly influential 1997 book *The Living Company* posed a simple question: What if we thought about a company as a living being? De Geus concluded that it would have a profound effect on the way we understand management.

For de Geus, the implications are enormous: 'If companies are living systems then the goals change. Living systems do not live to maximize shareholder value. They live to survive and to increase the potential of their components because that is how they increase their own potential.'

It's a concept that finds support from other commentators. In his book *Surfing the Edge of Chaos*, Richard Pascale explores the links between complexity theory, living organisms and modern organizations. 'The living organization is reality,' he says, 'the real metaphor is the mechanistic view of organizations.'

At the heart of the living company are what are increasingly recognized as an organization's most important assets – its people. The phrase 'people are our greatest asset' may be a cliché but it is also a truism.

In the twenty-first century it is people who create and sustain competitive advantage. Handling employees well is a prerequisite for a successful business strategy. So-called soft skills are growing in importance. Companies need to build commitment and trust; to repair the psychological contract between employer and employee.

Business leaders once regarded themselves as organizational engineers. The job was to ensure that the organizational machine was tuned up and pointing in the right direction. Today's CEOs are more akin to anthropologists.

Bill Critchley, business director of Ashridge Consulting, has researched what happens to new CEOs. 'What we're finding supports the emerging view of organizations as complex social processes, rather than machines,' he notes. 'This view suggests that organizations are inherently unpredictable. This challenges the conventional view, which was based on a cybernetic approach to organizations that has dominated since Frederick Taylor. It was an engineering view that suggested they could be controlled like a heating system.'

'But as the world becomes more complex, as communication increases exponentially, the view that the CEO can control the organization unravels. There used to be a view that you could set a five year strategy and prescribe behaviour to get there. Now we know that it doesn't work like that. If this organizational model is flawed then leaders have to give up trying to control people. They need to create the conditions to help people deal with the inherent uncertainty, and to be innovative in their responses.'

Companies are not philanthropic organizations. They are unlikely to pursue altruistic policies simply because people have feelings. But in a knowledge economy, employees are a scarce resource, and they vote with their feet. London Business School academic Sumantra Ghoshal talks about employees as 'volunteer investors' – independent and mobile; if not treated well, they will invest their talents elsewhere. In the twenty-first century companies can no longer afford to neglect the needs, aspirations and talents of their people.

DERRICK BELL: THE ARDENT PROTESTOR

Derrick Bell is one of America's most forthright and best-known commentators on race and ethics. A prolific author, his autobiography is entitled Confronting Authority: Reflections of an Ardent Protestor *and his latest book is called* Ethical Ambition *(Bloomsbury, 2002). Bell, now visiting professor at New York University's School of Law, attracted headlines when he became the first tenured black professor at Harvard Law School in 1971, only to leave in protest about the lack of black women on the faculty. He also resigned as dean of Oregon Law School after the school refused to hire a qualified Asian American woman.*

In this interview, Derrick Bell talks about the ethical questions now facing the corporate world in the wake of Enron, WorldCom and other scandals.

As a lawyer and academic, people might question your credentials to talk about business ethics.

True. It's one thing to preach about living an ethical life in the world of academia – sure there's some power plays there, and politics – but it's nothing like business. People might say what do I know about this slug-it-out, beat-to-the-bottom-line, winner-take-all world. I have avoided working within it.

But it seems to me that the principals are similar. You won't succeed unless your primary concern is keeping hold of your integrity. So you're right to think that this field of business is different, but I don't think it is possible to live a life without an ethical air. You need to look in the mirror.

So how can ambition be ethical? Aren't they mutually exclusive?

Ethics can be an integral part of your ambition. There is no lasting success that isn't ethically founded.

Ethical ambition means simultaneously honouring our values, our dreams and our needs. It requires critical compassion and honesty toward ourselves and others. It can be achieved only by thoughtfully and candidly assessing who we are, what we believe, what we value and what we desire. It also involves sacrifice – not only of time and energy, but of inaccurate or outdated perceptions of ourselves and our lives. Many of us are thwarted in achieving our goals because when our values and desires clash, we are paralysed. Others are disappointed with their lives because they surrender things – like hopes and convictions – that seemed to stand in the way of more material goals.

There are no universal codes of ethics are there? Nepotism, for example, is acceptable in Mexico but not in the US.

That's a good example because nepotism leads to its own difficulties inevitably, even if no laws are broken and some of it works out OK. I guess the Ford family is a good example though there are always exceptions. Basically, if you bring people in and shoot them up to the top there are negative reverberations all the way down. We're dealing with this in the White House; someone who, but for his father, would still be running losing businesses and now he is running the country.

You didn't vote for George Bush?

My vote for Ralph Nader probably helped to put him in!

Looking back at your career have you always looked in the mirror?

Of course, when I look back there were times when I thought I was doing right. At one point I was handling hundreds of school segregation suits and my marriage was probably a little shaky because my family hardly ever saw me. I was saving the world so far as I could see.

As I look back over those years I think, why didn't I recognize that I wasn't the white knight riding into town filing these suits? What I was doing was taking away leadership opportunities from people who were pretty much sidetracked waiting for this litigation to happen.

If some of the executives who are in so much trouble had been able to look in the mirror then they might have had a sense that it was not only wrong, but would lead to disaster.

But isn't greed central to capitalism?

Perhaps there's a word which is a little more subtle! There was a guy, who I talk about in my book, who was determined to avoid the rat race of the big law firms even though he had spectacular credentials and he joined a firm that had a reputation for treating people well. He did well there but he realized that although he hadn't intended it, over time his primary goal became making money. That was the measure. He warned people about this.

It is the subtle things. You're doing the same job each time and you can do it in 15 minutes rather than an hour but still bill an hour. Little things like that build up and build up. It's impressive but discouraging. It happens all the time. The secretaries who help themselves to stamps and paper. A small thing. But you'd really feel better about yourself buying your own goddamned pencils!

The question is good and my answer, though not very satisfying, is my answer. You don't have to sacrifice your integrity. When you do, even if it works and no one catches you, there is a price to pay.

Is too much emphasis now given to shareholder value?

Placing a high priority on shareholder value, while seemingly a valid basis for corporate policymaking, all too frequently serves as a shield for actions that, at best, are unethical and, at worse, criminal. The dealings include mergers like the hotly contested combining of Hewlett-Packard and Compaq, the principal benefit of which, according to opponents, will be increased profit through the dismissal of thousands of employees, and exorbitant payments to the top executives of the merging companies. With no apparent shame or remorse, businesses are setting up headquarters in Bermuda and other offshore locales, as the toolmaker Stanley Works is attempting to do, so as to avoid US taxes. To compete effectively, we are told, corporate America must move its manufacturing plants to third world countries to exploit low labour rates and, coincidentally, take advantage of lax health and environmental laws.

But don't such measures benefit shareholders?

These, and far more complicated tactics, often serve to benefit company executives while placing shareholders at risk. The various manoeuvres of Enron, aided and abetted by a major accounting company, Arthur Andersen, are examples of strategies that are hugely profitable for a time and then, when uncovered, are devastating to both employees and shareholders. The executives, unless indicted and convicted (quite difficult under United States laws) walk away perhaps chastened, but still very rich.

Shareholder value then is more a diversionary mantra then a guiding principle of many American corporations. Rather, the guiding principle is profit – however gained – that by the very nature of our free enterprise system, particularly when government oversight is deregulated or rendered ineffective by political inaction and inadequate funding of regulatory agencies, transforms reasonably honest business leaders into unbridled money-grubbers. Business executives of great intelligence, substantial business experience, and great wealth, involve themselves in financial schemes that are not only unethical, but downright stupid.

Could you give me an example?

Consider, former Alco International executive, L. Dennis Kozlowski, successful and rich beyond the wildest dreams of the average citizen, who now faces criminal prosecution for shipping expensive art objects intended for his Fifth Avenue apartment to New Hampshire to avoid the New York State sales tax. WorldCom's blatantly obvious accounting of expenses as profits, has upset even President Bush who has tried to distance himself from questionable shareholding practices not unlike those in which he himself was once involved. Then there is Martha Stewart, an icon of propriety, who has seen the stock in her business lose 39 per cent of its value in the wake of charges that she, a former stockbroker, used insider information to sell 4000 shares of ImClone stock one day before the company made an announcement that sent its share price plummeting.

What can be done?

As the scandals grow in number and in their blatant character, it is reasonable to ask whether anything can and should be done to clean up corporate America. The answer, beyond disgrace for those apprehended and small reforms in regulatory laws, is very little. Major corporations control the lives of ordinary citizens far more than the officials they elect and those officials, with very few exceptions, are beholden to corporations for the funds that keep them in office – a goal evidently far more important to most of them than either personal integrity or making good on the promises made when they were running for office. Aware that elections apparently have little to do with the important aspects of their lives, most people don't vote, and those who do are likely influenced more by TV advertisements – sponsored indirectly by major corporations – than by any careful and independent assessment of the candidates' records.

And truth be told, many working class Americans themselves, caught up in the hope that through the lottery or some other similarly unlikely scheme they will become rich, tend to admire as much as despise corporate corruption. When even the death of John Gotti, a notorious crime boss, captures the headlines, the interest and – let us say it – the admiration of the masses, public anger at wrongdoing in the executive suites is likely to be both minimal and brief.

And the solution?

There is no easy solution to an economic system that, while encouraging hard work, innovation and risk-taking in the quest for financial success, develops in some the sense that becoming number one is more important than how you get there. There is, though, a challenge for those who view the maintenance of ethical standards for themselves and their companies as not only the prudent course, but the only means of achieving a success unburdened by lies, cover-ups, and the continuing fear that structures built with greed as the glue will come undone. For the rest of us, we can speak out against corporate corruption, encourage those reforms that can be enacted, and support those who find the courage to reveal what they know is wrong.

If, despite the best efforts of expensive lawyers, friendly politicians, and high-powered public relations experts, the corporate scandals manage to generate widespread disgust and a demand for action, perhaps reform advocates can establish a corporate truth and reconciliation commission. In lieu of prosecution, business executives might be offered the chance to explain in detail how they evolved from ambitious and perhaps ethical young business people to the persons capable of the acts of which they are charged. If the testimony is forthright, society may gain an understanding of how success comes to be measured by wealth, power, and influence, rather than the commitment to integrity based on respect for self and others that at some point gets jettisoned as the price of getting ahead.

Has the world become overly materialistic?

Material success has replaced justice and equality as the overarching social goal. On one hand, because many obvious barriers to outsider success – overt and legally sanctioned prejudice – have been lifted or broken, material success *is* possible for those who only a generation or two ago might have had to put most of their energy into merely surviving. On the other hand, we still live in a society where racism, sexism, homophobia and other group prejudices remain viable despite the public rhetoric to the contrary. In fact, huge disparities in income and opportunity are generally accepted because we believe that those who work hard make it and those who don't, do not – we even believe it to a certain level when we're working hard and not making it! All of this creates profound stress because those of us who survive the challenges often feel that we must constantly choose between our beliefs and our goals, and end up either feeling guilty for succeeding or morally intact but personally unfulfilled.

People have been talking about ethics and codes of behaviour for decades. There is greater awareness but it isn't necessarily practiced.

I have no doubt we are going to have some stronger rules. But the ideal set of rules to keep money out of politics and so on aren't going to be developed in a few days. Those who feel strongly need to campaign for reform.

The major beneficiaries of higher ethical standards would be business because it would build confidence and what have you but they do not see that.

So in the short term, the number of abuses and examples of whistle blowing is likely to grow?

Yes, with whistle blowing people tend to remember the guys who come out looking great and are heralded, but the overall record is not good. They get fired, don't get much recompense, can't prove their case, and then can't find another job very easily.

There is an undercurrent of pessimism in your work – for example, regarding racism as a permanent aspect of the American and human condition.

It is a pessimistic aspect but a friend of mine has a disease and he says you have to learn how to die in order to learn how to live.

Basically, you have to recognize you aren't going to be here forever. That's the pessimistic thing – gee, I'm going to die. Then you move from that.

The other example I always use is Alcoholics Anonymous, where one of the first rules is that you get up and say that you are an alcoholic. It seems pessimistic but it is a realistic statement and you go from there. What can I do today? The road to optimism is paved with pessimism.

Would you describe yourself as an idealist?

At one time I would have, but now I realize that although idealism is worthwhile, it doesn't necessarily get you off the dime; when you look about it can keep you sitting down and not actually doing it. I think it is the recognition that what you're doing, particularly if it's tough, is likely not to be a success. And you do it because it's right to do it. It's the hope that it might happen. You tip your hat to the ideal.

You talk about the importance of character yet that is established by your genes?

You say so but you have the Hitlers and such who come out of backgrounds that wouldn't seem to offer anything.

Martin Luther King Jr. had a middle-class life all set up for him. His father was a well-known preacher. He was going to head back and take over his father's church when he stepped down. His character was changed by the dynamics of the protest movement which he was thrust into. He wasn't perfect but I don't suppose Jesus was perfect either.

So I think that character can change for the better but also for the worse.

Do you apply that to your own career and the stands you have taken?

I think so. It's a question of having models of people who have done things and you think 'Would I do that?' And then you look from that to what you are concerned about and it seems very small and a little easier to go against the grain and do it.

Would you still describe yourself as an ardent protestor?

Yes, probably. The dean just told all the faculty about some new appointments and I couldn't help myself from telling him that some of us weren't happy because they were all white. I do still get angry and fired up.

What should leaders like the dean be doing?

He said it was a high priority and, in truth, NYU does a lot better than other major schools. But they should look beyond traditional criteria, the feeling that you don't deserve to be here unless you were top of your class, clerked at the Supreme Court, have written articles and so on. By those criteria I wouldn't be here. The trouble is that people recruit in their own image or the image they think they have. They need to go beyond that.

Are you optimistic that progress will continue to be made or have things stalled?

Many of these things start off in a dramatic way of black and white but then evolve into other groups. Corporations now embrace diversity in its larger definition. White women have been the real beneficiaries of affirmative action in our country.

There is dramatic change in some areas. Things kind of go in waves and that's true in the racial diversity though the waves are not necessarily motivated by the highest principals but they're cyclical.

You are amazingly prolific: how do you divide your time?

I work all the time. I will be 72 this year and I probably work as hard as I did when I was 35 or 40. I look back on some of my hobbies and think how did I find the time to do that? I'm one of the fortunate ones in that everything I do – and I probably do too much – I enjoy.

JONAS RIDDERSTRÅLE: EMOTIONAL CAPITAL

Jonas Ridderstråle is best known as one half of the Swedish duo who brought the world the bestseller Funky Business *(FT.com, 2000). He is a professor at the Stockholm School of Economics but, shaven-headed and dressed in black, he is not your standard business school professor or management guru.*

When it appeared in 2000, Funky Business *struck a chord with managers. For some, the book became a bible of how to think about the bright new high-tech economy. Others dismissed the book for its lack of practical advice and for being a creature of its time.*

While commentators continue to debate the merits of Funky Business, *Jonas Ridderstråle and his long-time collaborator, Kjell Nordström, have continued to travel the world calling on businesses and managers to revolutionize their behaviour.*

Your book was criticized by some for not being practical enough. What practical advice do your ideas offer?

I think we are actually highly practical. We make it clear that success is dependent on getting the right people on board, formulating a great purpose, building world class processes, having clear priorities, infusing passion into the organization and being persistent. There is no quick fix to success. Smart, hard work has always and will always pay off.

An old fashioned message.

Yes, but people tended to assume that *Funky Business* was all about the new economy. It wasn't. In fact, our ideas are about how businesses will survive and thrive in the future.

What does a corporation need to equip itself with to succeed tomorrow?

First, you need speed. Velocity is a function of mass and energy. The lower the mass and the greater the energy, the higher the velocity.

During the last 20 years or so, businesses have been obsessed with reducing their mass. They have outsourced, re-engineered, and downsized desperately. What they have forgotten about is the other part of the equation: energy. The time has come for companies to stop re-engineering and to start re-energizing.

How do you re-energize an organization?

For a start you need to change the debate – companies talk a lot about core competencies but they are meaningless without core compassion, actually caring about what you do, why you do it and who you do it with. Organizations can start by hiring people with a passion for their business. In reality, companies actually steer clear of passionate people. They would rather hire dull, reliable people than passionate enthusiasts with an appetite for change. They fill their ranks with people who want the future to be the same rather than people who want to invent the future. One thing we can be sure of is that the future will not bring more of the same.

So companies have to get in touch with people's emotions?

Yes, they must excite, energize and enthuse competent individuals. They must understand that what they sell and what their customers buy are quite often two very different things. A Harley-Davidson executive observed that the company offers a 43-year-old accountant to dress in black leather, ride through small towns and have people be afraid of him. Harley-Davidson is selling motorbikes but it is also selling dreams.

The very nature of competition has changed. It used to be a question of products. Then it became products plus services. Now, we are in the business of creating an emotional experience. We have moved from a world of things that you can touch into one where it's a question of adding a human touch. Emotional experience is not a question of more logic, more reason. It is a question of affection, intuition, desire and lust.

You say that companies need to find 'temporary monopolies'. What do you mean?

For a short moment in time or space you must be unique. From this perspective, there is no difference between Microsoft and Madonna, Palm Pilot and Pablo Picasso. So companies have to be innovative in unexpected ways. The unknown and the unseen do not have any competitors.

Think about why Nokia is so successful. It does not possess groundbreaking technology that its competitors cannot get hold of. But it has realized that competitive advantage is about more than having great technology, the best organized company, or the best suppliers. These are all essential, but they don't give you an advantage because your competitors will be doing much the same.

Competitive advantages must be created elsewhere. You need to create a culture of passion promoting fantasy and feelings – ideas and imagination. It works because while copying a product is easy, copying a culture of passion such as Nokia's is all but impossible.

What is the lesson we should learn from the dot-com meltdown?

A bad idea does not become a stroke of genius just because you place it on the Web. Business boils down to making money – having more revenues than costs. To ensure this you need a temporary monopoly. Behind these monopolies there must be a unique innovation of some sort – not just another vanilla-flavoured ice cream.

Companies are now told to nurture their most talented individuals. What about the average individuals? Won't this demotivate them?

The growing difference between the best and the rest is a fact of life. What is critical in many firms is not so much the core competencies as the 'core competents' – the individuals who make competencies happen. These are the limited number of people at an organization who actually embody the skills that make the products and services unique – Bill Joy of Sun Microsystems and Brian Wilson of the Beach Boys. We find these knowledge nomads all over the map. We find them in sports – the Liverpool soccer team with or without Michael Owen. We find them in media – CNN and Larry King. We find them in business – Bill Gates once claimed that if 30 people were to leave Microsoft, the company would risk bankruptcy.

Will ordinary people put up with this? Can a high-performance organization include both talent and the merely average? I think so. Consider sports. The highest paid player in the baseball team New York Yankees, short-stopper Derek Jeter, earns some $12.6 million per year. The lowest paid guy, D'Angelo Jimenez, also a short-stopper, gets a paltry $200,000 every year. The team has won four of the last six World Series. The question of what society this development leads to, however, is a quite different one.

You argue that nation states are no longer important. Can you explain?

We're entering a tribal world. We all grew up in a world in which geography mattered and physical proximity ruled. So, the tribe of yesterday was geographically structured: Americans, Armenians, Australians and Argentinians. The new tribes, I believe, will be biographically structured – hip-hopers, Amnesty International members, and so on – made up of people who actually feel that they have something in common, no matter where they were born.

What are the implications for companies?

Smart companies realize that they must build an organizational tribe where people share common traits or interests – whether it is ownership, culture, attitude or whatever. Increasingly, values will constitute the lowest common denominator that keeps the community together. As the easiest way to get people to share your values is to hire people who already do, more organizations now recruit people with the right attitude, then train them in the skills they need. They simply do not believe in the idea of bringing in smart people and then brainwashing them at training camps. The reality is that if you recruit someone with relevant knowledge today, three months down the road these skills may be obsolete. And it is easier to change our skills than our basic values.

LEIF EDVINSSON: THE CONTEXT'S THE THING

Leif Edvinsson's business card labels him a 'global knowledge nomad'. The restlessly peripatetic Swede is a former winner of the 'Brain of the Year' award. Edvinsson came to prominence as the world's first director of intellectual capital at the insurance company Skandia. He is the author of Intellectual Capital *(with Michael Malone) and* Corporate Longitude.

Having left Skandia in 1999, Edvinsson is an adjunct professor in Knowledge Economics at Lund University and is involved with Sweden's Royal Institute of Technology which is offering a new degree in design and health delivered in Sweden and Italy.

Leif Edvinsson talks about twenty-first century knowledge work.

What is the big issue currently occupying your mind?

The big issue now is the context around the knowledge worker. The context surrounding knowledge workers has become tougher. Research suggests that 20 per cent of our health is related to the architecture which surrounds us – work space design, sound levels, smells, types of seating and so on. Context matters. That's why VW Audi has a seven-man research team looking into the smell of new cars. It is part of the image of the car. When someone buys a car they want the smell of high quality leather rather than glue or oil. The same goes for attracting knowledge workers to a job. They require the right context.

One of the things I like to do is to have meetings while walking. It is more enjoyable and more fertile. Do you really think that sitting in an airless, windowless office is the best environment to come up with great ideas?

And if you get the context wrong?

People suffer from burn-out. Companies cut numbers so that fewer people are expected to work harder and harder. The end result is the anorexic corporation. Every 15 minutes someone succumbs to burn-out in Sweden alone. This is incredibly costly as companies lose human and structural capital. At society level wealth creation is consequently slowing down at a huge social cost.

While it takes weeks to chemically treat cancer, burn-out takes much longer to treat. We spend about one tenth of what we spend on medical treatment on the context of knowledge workers. Yet the context has a much bigger impact.

This is not just a Swedish problem. In Japan there is *karoshi* – death by overwork – and working hours in the US are significantly higher than those in Europe. We are working harder rather than smarter. We now need to focus on knowledge care in terms of the context as well as the brain itself.

So the challenge of intellectual capital is also very personal and health-oriented. One important dimension of this is to replace offices with other meeting places or knowledge arenas, such as knowledge cafés. We have to have space to clear our heads to seize our own opportunities. In years gone by, people took the waters in search of physical restoration. Now, we need mental spas, places where we can renew ourselves and our minds. After all, we have the potential for hundreds of billions of thoughts per day.

The opportunity cost of not seizing these opportunities is enormous. This is brain economics; the care for the talent potential. I think it was Peter Drucker who lamented the inefficiency of the knowledge worker. He was right. You, as brainpower, can work positively and usefully for 4–8 hours per day. Thereafter, your effect is likely to be a negative one.

So, the questions we should be asking are: how can the brains of people operate to their best? How do we design working life as well as we do our cities?

There is a security dimension to this: what I call the defence of intellectual capital. How do you create a secure environment for your knowledge recipes? How do you avoid detrimental hackers to your IT systems? How do you protect the health of vital knowledge workers? The question of the defence of intellectual capital is, at the moment, in the hands of very few people.

In your brain there is something called the hippocampus, which is your intelligence centre. This screens the signals from the surrounding context. From this, the brain produces adrenaline or serotonin which produces a happy smile. Business leaders need to ask: how can they produce a context that has a positive impact on people's hippocampus? At a time of uncertainty, leaders have to act as catalysts, have the courage to prototype, to probe, then to use their sensitivity and intelligence and then to act. We have to move from reactive behaviour – such as budget planning – to prototyping, experimenting, acting as a catalyst. People in organizations just don't do it because they're scared. They block themselves. So the leadership focus should be on creating the context to give people the confidence as well as mind satisfaction.

What can companies do?

They need to continuously invite new solutions which are just around the corner, waiting to be applied. They need speed and even more rhythm. In times of uncertainty they need to come up with more innovations, answers to the unknown. At a practical level, they can change the reception area, as Skandia did, into a welcoming space like a bar, instead of the traditional gatekeeping design. If they're a museum, take away the ticket office. Open up. Security is a paradox. On one hand it is about locking things up – like protecting patents. But from an economic and psychological perspective, you have to move to a defence based on opening up rather than locking up. The trend now is to close doors rather than encouraging transparency. It is counter-productive.

Companies can change working contracts so they employ more part-time people to reduce stress and increase people's intelligence by providing new perspectives. They can invite senior citizens into the organization because they have a different perspective. They can scale down to work with fission rather than fusion; they can use a federal structure rather than focusing on mergers and acquisitions.

Finally, companies should develop contexts, connections and contactivity to leverage the intellectual capital in waiting around the business.

Intellectual capital measures are now also applied to nations. Is this useful?

The intellectual capital of nations is becoming more important. Today most nations are not leveraging their brainpower, but rather burning it out. They are approaching a new risk level of poverty rather than wealth. There are four main enablers for future wealth, according to the Canadian Nick Bontis, in reverse order of importance – business efficiency, foreign trade, education and R&D. That's the intellectual capital agenda for nations. R&D and education are by far the most important. We are currently investing a lot in military R&D. The good news from this is that it will have – at some stage – a positive impact for society with spin-offs in technology, medical treatment, healthcare and food. Technological investments in defence have often been a key driver for the development of structural capital.

At the same time, we need new organizational models. If schooling is so important to society, what kind of schools or universities could we develop? If R&D is important, what new arenas for experimentation could be developed? If demographics show a greying workforce, what kind of initiatives can we take to offer senior citizens new opportunities? If 20 per cent of the world's brains are in Asia – where China is graduating the same number of MScs annually as the US has a total stock – what kind of cultural bridges do we need to develop between Asia and Europe?

What other trends do you envisage?

Another is the rise of knowledge tourism. Knowledge tourists spend ten times more than a traditional tourist. Thousands of Japanese visit Sweden every year just to look at Swedish houses for senior citizens. The next area might be to visit laboratories and other mind-stimulating spaces.

We are going to see intelligent cities as well as regions – look at Bangalore in India or Sophia Antipolis in France. Barcelona already has a chief knowledge officer to develop the city's intellectual capital. In the old days, harbours were for the movement of goods; now we need harbours for the flow of knowledge.

Oil is the current battlefield. In the future it might be brainpower. We are moving from oil power to brainpower. So how is your hippocampus doing now?

TONY BUZAN: BRAIN POWER

It is easy to forget that Tony Buzan is a busy man. The Renaissance man responsible for over 80 books, a business empire and a legion of other activities, sits in a tracksuit amid the clutter of his studio overlooking the Thames near Marlow. The 60-year-old Buzan has completed his morning's rowing – a sport at which he is an Olympic coach – and is ready for the working day, a day diligently plotted out in his self-designed diary. His rowing performance has already been immaculately entered into his records.

Buzan is best known as the creator of Mind Mapping®, a 'thinking tool' once described, colourfully and not altogether helpfully, as the 'Swiss army knife of the brain'. A mind map is a kind of mental shorthand. Arguments and ideas radiate in tentacles from a centre point.

Buzan – as he well knows – is the best advertisement for the practical usefulness of his ideas. He lives his theories. His central argument is that the magical powers of the human brain remain largely untapped. Our greatest asset is allowed to wallow in ill-organized, poorly-directed lethargy. Unused muscles rapidly lose their tone.

Recent corporate trends, such as knowledge management and the growing interest in intellectual capital, suggest to Buzan that the tide is turning. Companies and managers are suddenly interested in harnessing the intellects as well as the muscles of their people.

Do you think your views have suddenly become accepted as mainstream?

Undoubtedly, there is growing attention on the brain. It is becoming the world's number one focus of attention.

In September 1991, *Fortune* published a cover picture of the left and right sides of the brain. The heading was 'Brain power'. It was the first time a magazine had used a brain as the front cover. I started collecting magazine covers featuring the brain and now have over 150 covers. The brain has become a way to sell magazines.

The *Fortune* article was the first sensible article in a business magazine about the fundamental worth of a worker and recognition of what a worker does. It has taken another ten years for it to become generic. And that's fast.

Has it taken you by surprise?

When you know the power of the brain it is blindingly obvious.

What was the genesis of your thinking?

At university I increasingly found it difficult to finish big essays. There was so much knowledge. I was interested in everything so couldn't see why I couldn't study everything. It was like confetti and I wanted to grab it in a way that gave it an organized structure. And then I began to develop mind mapping.

One of the things I did was to design my own diary, which I still use. At the beginning of the year I plan out the main areas of activity. It is knowledge management. If you're going to manage knowledge, the first thing you have to manage is the knowledge manager and that is the brain. If you manage it then it manages itself. It is a self-managing system but needs the correct formula if it is to be managed. It needs the correct software programs. I work out at the beginning of the year how many times I will lecture and so on. Then I look at the months. Everything's colour co-ordinated.

As well as the diary, I captured the data at university through mind mapping.

What's the reasoning behind mind maps?

Knowledge is not linear. A book is not linear. All kinds of things radiate from your head when you have an idea. It is like an explosion, a supernova. It is in 360 degrees, three dimensions. That's what a mind map helps to capture.

A kind of mental shorthand?

Yes. One page of A4 can become a 100-page report. If I come back to a mind map in 20 years, I will know instantly what it was about. It is the visualization of thought. Without them I'd struggle.

Isn't it overly organized? Don't you have to be a control freak to organize your life and mind to the extent you suggest?

It doesn't feel organized. It is a natural expression of my self-organizing system.

But how far ahead do you plan?

I plan beyond the end of my life and then go back from that. I plan comfortably a year ahead, two really. I plan at the end and beginning of the day. I don't plan weekly, but daily and monthly.

I'm very much not a control freak. I'm flexible in changing what I've decided if it fits in with my goals. Planning is not control. If I'm thinking ten years ahead, it is a freedom. Freedom to make my own decisions and enjoy myself.

How does this method of organizing your activities link to how things are organized more generally?

The traditional concept of organization is often desperately close to rigidification and compartmentalization rather than integration.

The brain is self-organizing. It's designed to organize and manage knowledge. It has astonishing power to do that. It is, in part, a blank slate. If you feed it the incorrect formula it will organize itself in that way. This will lead to disorganization.

I was one of the best note-takers in school and university. We took standard linear notes and were trained to use certain ink, Quink blue-black. A blue or a black is monochrome, a monotone is monotonous and dull. The bulk of the literate population is taking notes in terms of knowledge management which send them to sleep and which may bring only a small fraction of what the brain needs. It was a long, painful and very exciting discovery.

Can you explain what happened?

It used to take me three months to do a 5000-word essay. That was a lot of writing and rewriting and was the same for the other students. If a writer writes 500 words a day then they're pleased. It made sense to me, but then I thought that was a page and a bit, four minutes of talking. Then I began to see that it was utterly insane. In writing, my function is to transfer what I know from my head onto the page. I learned to type and got up to 70 words per minute. My fingers were tripping over my thoughts all the time. I thought there must be a faster way.

What is the fastest most durable muscle in my body? The tongue. I took mind maps and taped what I would have typed. I have a mind map for a book surrounded by other mind maps. I spend two days getting myself into writing/grammatical mode – as we never speak in grammar mode. I then translate the mind maps into text.

My average writing per day is 10,000 to 20,000 words. It doesn't feel fast. The mind map is the framework. I don't need to change it. It is the thinking that leads to the mind map. When I'm writing, I have a mind map in my head. I describe it. I know how many words I put down – 140–150 words a minute. Give me 30 minutes and I know how much I can produce.

And your production rate has been staggering – over 80 books. Why this staggering flow of words?

I'm increasing my output because I've got so many things to say. When you know the potential of the brain, it's profound and profoundly important. But if you've never been taught about your brain all you know is that your brain is your real problem. It is three pounds of grey slush and you're losing brain cells and your memory's going. People don't like their brains; they've been taught the formula that colour, imagination and daydreaming are wrong and childish. So when someone comes along and says you need to use colour and be playful, the immediate reaction is that they're talking nonsense. It's not just teaching people how to do it. It is removing the blindness with which people have been brought up.

What's the business case for the brain?

In the mid-1970s, after the TV programme *Use Your Head*, I gave a presentation to a group of senior executives. One of them said that it was really fascinating but what has the brain got to do with business? I recommended he went into his business and extracted the brains to have his answer.

Imagine a company that is just the same as your own, a clone which opens up across the road. Each of the individuals in the newly cloned company is 10 per cent more intelligent, 10 per cent more fit, 10 per cent faster in everything they do that requires speed, 10 per cent healthier, 10 per cent less stressed, 10 per cent better at learning and thinking, 10 per cent more energetic, and 10 per cent happier. How long would it take for the clone to dominate? What would happen to the other company? It wouldn't last long. The thing is that it is quite easy to become the alternative company.

Isn't there a danger that knowledge management and intellectual capital will become yet more short-lived management fads?

Yes, it's a major danger. Companies follow the fad because it's the route to competitive advantage. But they don't go deeper to what originated the fad in the first place. Whatever the fad, what is the first thing companies have to teach their people? The first thing is to be able to learn and to be able to remember what they have learned. They have to learn to think and create and then apply it all to make some money. The trouble is that they don't do any of it.

And yet companies invest more than ever in training and developing people.

To lose £800,000 in a day, invest £1 million in training – 80 per cent of what people learn is forgotten within a day of training. That isn't because training is inappropriate, it is because the training doesn't take into account the brain. Until training takes the brain into account, they'll continue to have new fads and new titular directors of the fads. They will continue to be disillusioned and search for the perfect fad, the panacea. The good news is that business schools now often include mind mapping as part of their teaching equipment.

Have companies put your ideas into practice?

One of the most memorable examples was the accounts department of IBM in New York. They structured their activities through mind maps. This saved the company millions of dollars and made them money. They trained their people how to think.

At another company, all the departments mind mapped their functions then looked at strengths, weaknesses and needs and opinions of the other departments. Then they were all brought together and looked at the mind map and saw opportunities for synergy, for joint handling of some projects and sharing of responsibilities. In some areas, a 10 per cent rate of errors was reduced to 0.5 per cent. The time taken to complete certain tasks was reduced from 10 hours to 2.

One organization I have worked with is the Lichenstein Global Trust, which is a $50 billion bank with about 1000 people. Half of them have now been trained – an average of four weeks each. The training covers the mind and the body – they're taught about mind mapping, innovation, creativity, knowledge management, communication skills, poetry to strengthen their metaphorical muscle, aerobic fitness, ikedo, rowing, and mind sports like chess and the Japanese board game goh. This has transformed the company's culture, personal and family lives. People are healthier and communications skills have been notably enhanced.

So the power of the brain is accessible to everyone rather than a select few?

Yes, most people think that they're less able to determine their own future than they really are. People think they're trapped when they are not. It is self-perpetuating until you get a bigger perspective. Once you realize you are trapped, you change.

I worked out a criteria for genius for a book I wrote. I was annoyed that genius was seen as a very rare gift. In most of the texts it is defined as indefinable. I studied the lives of geniuses and found absolute criteria. I couldn't find a genius without 100 per cent of the criteria.

My favourite was da Vinci. I thought that he was some way out on top, but he came top just ahead of Goethe. It was a journey of self-awareness. Your own knowledge banks explode. Rather than living in their little tunnels alone, they were passionate, lusty, super physical – virtually the opposite of their public image.

How would you describe yourself?

I think as a poet, author and businessman. Holanthropy is a word I have devised – the study of the mind and body, intra- and interpersonal relationships.

MARSHALL GOLDSMITH: COACHING FOR RESULTS

Executive coaching is a huge growth market. With senior managers under increasing pressure from investors, analysts and a host of others, and CEO tenure plummeting, executives appear desperate for help. Enter the coach.

Marshall Goldsmith is one of the world's best-known – and best-paid – executive coaches. Ranked among the top ten executive educators by the Wall Street Journal, *recent profiles in the* New Yorker *and the* Harvard Business Review *confirm his place at the top of his chosen profession. Goldsmith's reputation is based on results.*

In support of business leaders he has racked up an impressive 7 million air miles and coached over 50 major CEOs. His books include Coaching for Leadership *and* The Leader of the Future. *Hyperactive and relentlessly positive, Goldsmith is based in California. Goldsmith's coaching methodology is now being used by Hewitt Associates, the largest executive coaching firm in the world.*

When did the executive coaching take off, and how has it evolved in recent years?

It started about ten years ago, but it really took off in the last five. If you look back through history I'm sure great leaders had someone who acted as a coach – so it's not a new idea. But it is still a relatively unsophisticated field.

One problem is that executive coaching is growing while therapy and other fields are shrinking. This has encouraged some people to move out of those areas into coaching. Coaching is huge at the moment. There is a bandwagon effect. Coaching will remain but I wouldn't expect the bandwagon to continue indefinitely. It will fall back.

Can you mass-produce coaching? Isn't it a very personal, one-to-one experience?

We teach our clients to learn from their people. We've trained people at GE Capital in my coaching methods and the results are just as good as using external coaches. The key is that the coach is not an expert but a facilitator.

The coach is usually seen as a physician who can cure all known ills. Our method is not about that. What people learn is a process.

How does someone go about finding and hiring the right coach? What are the pitfalls?

You should ask a coach what they specialize at. Too many coaches will ask 'what is your problem?' and then say they can help. If a coach says he is an expert at seven things then you have to wonder how good he really is at number seven.

What do you specialize at?

I have a very narrow focus. I don't do life planning, career planning, strategy or personal productivity. I am the best in the world in my narrow area – or maybe second best. My specialism is interpersonal skills – behavioural issues. It's about finding the right coach for the issue.

How much depends on the coach and how much on the willingness of the executive to change?

A lot of people put all the attention on the coach. That's the wrong way round. It is the executive that is responsible for whether he changes or not. The same applies to training. A lot of training and executive education is a waste of time because the focus is on the people providing the programme rather than the participants. The problem with a lot of it is that the participants evaluate the trainers and consultants. The only people who learn from that are the trainers and consultants. It is the managers participating on the programmes that need to be evaluated to see if they have changed the way they do things.

How can you be sure that your coaching actually makes a difference?

Simple. I don't get paid if people don't change. Many other executive coaches have a conflict of interest when it comes to payments. They rely on the client liking them. They charge according to how much time they spend with the client.

Mine is a very novel pricing model but it is very easy to measure behavioural change – and executives like it because our pay is linked to results. We get people to say that they will do X and Y and then we see if they have actually done it. Key to this is executive ownership. That is ten on a scale of importance while pleasing psychologists is zero.

What happens when you go into an organization?

The first thing is that we only work with people if they agree to do certain things. We do a lot of customer qualification. If people don't want to do the things we ask, we won't work with them. The typical person we coach is stubborn. They think that they're right. In many ways, the worse they are the better.

We help develop a leadership inventory. Then we choose the key areas to change and agree those with the executive we're coaching. The executive will then talk to the people he or she works with to explain what they would like to change and that the past is passed. They say, 'what would you like me to do?' Obviously, they don't do everything that people suggest – leadership is not a popularity contest.

Talking to people who work with the executive, we then come up with measures. The important thing is that it is the people who work with the executive who come up with the measures.

The onus is on colleagues and co-workers to be involved?

Very much so. If you want a better relationship with your co-workers then the co-workers need to be coaches. We ask co-workers whether they can let go of the past. Next we ask whether they can commit to tell the truth. Then we ask whether they can be helpful to the person being coached rather than being cynical or sarcastic. Finally the co-worker has to think of something they can do better. 98% of people agree to do all of this.

How much time would you typically spend with a client?

I don't talk about the number of hours I spend with an executive. That's not important. I spend as little time as possible to get results. These people are expensive and their time is a valuable resource.

What happens after the initial agreement?

We have a dedicated follow-up process. After six months we will have a mini-survey of the person's behaviour over the previous six months. We expect people's behaviour to be better rather than perfect.

You make changing people's behaviour sound quite straightforward.

It is much harder to change perception than behaviour. The closer you are to a person, the less likely you are to believe that they will change. The most cynical people are the people you live with. At home they laugh in your face; at work they laugh behind your back.

Do cultural differences have an impact on the effectiveness of your method and of coaching in general?

No. The higher you go in organizations, the fewer cultural differences are encountered. How different are 35-year-old MBAs from each other? They have travelled and worked throughout the world and have good educational backgrounds.

A traditional coach sets himself up as an expert. We don't do that so that makes a difference. This is not life planning or career coaching. Most requests for coaching are about changing behaviour and that's what we're interested in.

Aren't coaches simply glorified psychologists, listening to the problems and deficiencies of executives?

In therapy it might take 20 years but we're not interested in peoples' psychological issues. We're simply concerned about how they behave at work.

Is the coach simply a sounding board?

I've heard people say that a great coach has no agenda. That's ridiculous.

In the literature it says that a coach is a good listener. There is no research to support this. My empathy gene was removed at birth, one article about me observed. It is not designed for my client to love me. I spend as little time as is necessary with my clients.

Isn't coaching simply a management fad which will disappear after a year or two?

Having a coach now has positive rather than negative status, but the popularity of coaching creates confusion about what coaching actually is. With our coaching there is a simple clear response: did people get better?

There will be a market shake out leaving a small group of companies who deliver results. Like any fad, there is a lack of definition in the coaching field. There are a lot of well intentioned people, a lot of charlatans and some who are good at what they do.

A lot of coaches say they can do anything. But the reality is that there are lots of different types of coaching. If you want coaching about strategy you don't come to me, you go to CK Prahalad. If you want life coaching you might go to Richard Leiter and so on. There is no generic model of the coach.

You need to figure out what you need and then find the right coach. If you don't know what kind of coach you need, you might as well say that you need a teacher. To teach you what?

KJELL NORDSTRÖM: TRIBAL GATHERING

Kjell Nordström is a striking figure. Even in a fashionable Stockholm restaurant where he is well known, heads turn on his entry. Tall, shaven-headed, dressed in black and with an array of jewellery, Nordström more closely resembles a rock star than the university academic he actually is.

He and his work reached a wider audience through the success of the book Funky Business *(FT.com 2000) which he co-authored with his colleague Jonas Ridderstråle.*

The book helped seal Nordström's reputation as one of Europe's leading business gurus and he now travels the world preaching his funky message. His seminars are sell-outs. Along the way, the academic has been turned into an entertainer as well as an educator. He talked in his minimalist Stockholm home.

You talk a lot about differentiation, but how should companies differentiate themselves?

The starting point must be a neat niche, a funky few, a global tribe. You need to understand your particular tribe better than anyone else. You must know what makes them tick, what scares them, what gets them out of bed in the morning, what turns them on. The tribe is the basic unit of business. If you don't know who your tribe is or anything about them, you are not going to stand out from the crowd.

The good news is that there are a lot of tribes out there – and some are enormous. It's just a question of identifying them, understanding them and meeting their needs better than anyone else. We recently came upon a great example of this in financial services. The American Steve Dunlap was refused a loan to build a resort for homosexuals. So he decided to establish the G&L Internet Bank. G stands for gay and L for lesbian. The basic idea is to target the 21 million or so American gays and lesbians – a group with a combined annual budget of some $800 billion.

Tribes come in a variety of shapes and forms. Pilgrims create tribes. Every year, 75,000 Chevrolet Suburban vans are sold in Saudi

Arabia as the pilgrims who visit Mecca are only allowed to enter the city in a vehicle with specific measurements. The only car that fits the specs happens to be the Chevrolet Suburban.

So what's the message?

If you focus your energy on creating and then exploiting an extremely narrow niche you can make a lot of money. The tribe may consist of one-legged homosexual dentists. It may be lawyers who race pigeons. But if you manage to capture these customers globally, you can make a lot of money. There are riches in niches.

You also talk of tribes within organizations. Isn't there a thin line between organizational tribes and brainwashing?

Tribes are filled with people who believe in what they're doing. For better or worse, loathe it or hate it, that's what they believe in. Brainwashing is about forcing people to believe something. So, the similarities are limited to non-existent.

But it is true that tribes require strong cultures. Or, as someone once said of Nike: 'It is like a cult – but it's a nice cult.' In a tribe people get energy from one another. The Zulu's have a word for it: 'ubuntu'. This can be translated as a person is a person because of other persons. Or as Jung put it: 'I need we to be fully I.' Tribal behaviour has to come from within.

For all the technology at our disposal, there is still the feeling that the results are impersonal and robotic. How do you move beyond that?

You have to make every interaction with consumers personal and highly human. Think emotional capital. Stir emotions in your consumers

To do so, you must focus on the extended experience. Try to look and think beyond the atoms, bits or search engines involved. As someone remarked, sushi is really cold, dead fish, but that isn't what the customer buys or how it should be marketed. The trouble is, many companies still persist in selling cold, dead fish to consumers who are much more interested in sushi.

This reasoning applies to all products. What do we really buy when we come home with a Nokia mobile phone, a pair of GAP khakis, or a Sony Walkman?

The moral is that what companies sell and what their customers buy are two different things. Therefore, every once in a while it is wise to place yourself in the shoes of your customers and ask the question: What are they really buying? The answer, 99 times out of 100, is not what you think you are selling. Then put yourself in their shoes once more and examine their interaction with you and your company. How does it strike their emotions? If it doesn't, think again.

You recommend that you recruit people who already have the right values, but how do you actually do this?

You're right. Our argument is that while there is a lot of mystification surrounding the subject of values, the simplest way to get people to share your values is to recruit people who already do. Herb Kelleher of SouthWest Airlines professes to hire attitudes rather than aptitudes. The logic is that you can make positive people into good pilots, but turning great pilots with attitude problems into charming servers of customers is close to impossible. Consequently, smart companies recruit people with the right attitude, then train them in the necessary skills – rather than the reverse. Just imagine Hell's Angels recruiting for skills instead of attitude. Lenin was right. Find the revolutionaries. Do not try to change people.

How you do it is not that hard. When you place ads, select people, interview people or whatever you do to recruit them, put questions about values to the top of the agenda. You can usually train people to do a job; but you can't change their minds so easily.

Aren't the mavericks you call on companies to recruit very difficult to manage?

Of course. In our gigs we use a picture of Richard Branson in a wedding dress. Too many companies are still turning down applications from Richard Branson types. They can't cope with difference. Some can't even contemplate difference.

If you want to find great people you've got to look in unusual places. Recruiting only from Harvard Business School or INSEAD, will result in a pretty homogeneous crowd. Cisco, for example, tries to find people at the Boston Marathon and the Mountain View International Microbrewery Festival. Mavericks rule. If you can't manage them, your competitors will.

What's going to happen to those who still aren't convinced by the advantages of technology?

Let's be absolutely clear about something: the global market economy of our times is neither good nor bad, right nor wrong – it just is. Market capitalism is a machine. But a machine does not have a soul. We have to develop this one together as we go along.

In order to get rid of that human shadow called poverty, we have to make up our minds as to what a good life is. Technology without ideology and values does not produce much value. As noted by Charles Handy, the market is not a substitute for responsibility – merely a mechanism for sorting the efficient from the inefficient.

The so-called digital divide is not a consequence of the technology as such, but rather of our inability to create a world where more people are given an opportunity to develop their talents. Never before in the history of mankind have we had so many potent tools that potentially enable us to build a better world and companies that are actually fun to work for, but it is up to us to create this future.

TOM STEWART: INTELLECTUAL CAPITALIST

Capital used to be viewed in physical, tangible terms – factories, machinery and money. Now the quest is on for greater understanding of the most intangible, elusive, mobile and important assets of all: intellectual capital.

Intellectual capital can be crudely described as the collective brainpower of an organization. The switch from physical assets to intellectual assets – brawn to brain – as the source of wealth creation has been underway in the developed economies for some time. As an advertisement for Deutsche Bank put it: 'Ideas are capital. The rest is just money'. Among the most influential chroniclers of this shift is Thomas A Stewart, author of The Wealth of Knowledge *and* Intellectual Capital: the New Wealth of Organizations. *Stewart, formerly a columnist with* Fortune, *became editor of the* Harvard Business Review *in Autumn 2002.*

Stewart claims that the changes taking place are as significant as the Industrial Revolution. 'Knowledge has become the most important factor in economic life. It is the chief ingredient of what we buy and sell, the raw material with which we work. Intellectual capital – not natural resources, machinery or even financial capital – has become the one indispensable asset of corporations,' he says.

Tom Stewart explains how converting knowledge into intellectual capital is a new and elusive form of corporate alchemy.

Your book cites Enron as an example of best practice. You were not alone in lauding the company's management practices. What do you now say?

Enron is an interesting story in a number of ways. This sort of misbehaviour comes about because people think they can get away with it and people are prepared to believe it. Frauds and bubbles do not occur independently of real opportunities. People sell patent medicines because there are real medicines. People invest in tulips because there is a world of opportunity.

Enron was, therefore, a perverse manifestation of real opportunities as well as being a cautionary tale. Enron reported business that wasn't there. Enron was a fiction but that doesn't mean that everything intangible is a fiction. One of the other things that Enron tried to do was to create markets in things that hadn't existed before. That is already happening elsewhere – in electricity for example. The fact that Enron inaccurately and deliberately misstated results from those markets does not change those underlying facts.

Enron should serve as a challenge. It shows that we really need to fix accounting. The inadequacies of traditional accounting allow people to get away with such things. Accounting needs reinvention as well as reform. Unfortunately, Enron may move things the other way.

There is a sense looking through your book and others on intellectual capital that only a small number of companies are making it work. The same names keep cropping up.

You'd always like to find brand new companies doing exceptionally interesting things. But over the years it tends to be a small number of companies, the usual suspects.

Intellectual capital is being implemented effectively by some companies. The Scandinavian countries, led by Denmark, are leading the way in terms of reporting intellectual capital. But knowledge management is being implemented inefficiently in a larger number of companies. To some extent, the intellectual capital agenda has been captured by knowledge management to the detriment of both.

The difference between knowledge management and intellectual capital is basically the same as the difference between management and capital. Management is something you do to get more out of capital. Knowledge management has become the domain of the technologists, which is useful but not the be-all and end-all.

Isn't intellectual capital in danger of becoming just another management fad?

Surviving fad-dom is not a trivial accomplishment. The definition of a fad is that people start doing something without having a reason for doing it. There was a study by Forrester Research that found that six out of seven companies undertaking knowledge management projects did not calculate return on investment. That's a definition of a fad.

More money has been wasted than made in knowledge management so far. When things go wrong it's usually because it has been introduced for faddish reasons. But increasingly I see companies looking first to discover their knowledge business, their knowledge value proposition – what they know they can sell and how to sell it profitably – and then figuring out how to manage knowledge. That approach works.

So, the faddishness is disappearing. You can see it in the diminishing advertising pages of knowledge management magazines. Going out and throwing technology at it is over. That's good because it creates the real opportunity, the opportunity that I write about: let's find the knowledge and build the organization around it to run a profitable knowledge business. Too many companies have seen knowledge as an internal matter, making sure that everyone knows what everyone else knows. All this is good, but to what end?

If knowledge management is something of a distraction, what should managers be looking at?

The real question is what is the knowledge business? And then, tracking the knowledge business, building and acquiring the assets needed to make the business more profitable and effective. The wealth of knowledge is not found internally but in the markets.

We need to look at what customers are buying and ask questions. Why are they shopping in our store? Why aren't they buying from the competition? What do people purchase from us that is unique and valuable? What is a customer paying for when he or she buys from us? The answer is a set of attributes and price – quality, breadth of product line, and so on. But what created that broad product line, technical expertise or quality? What allows companies to offer low prices? It's then you uncover knowledge, the knowledge assets that produce value.

Aren't knowledge management and intellectual capital fighting against human nature? People are simply not very good at sharing.

One of the big questions in an organization is how you get promoted. A lot of organizations that talk about knowledge reward people for hoarding rather than sharing it. Until you build knowledge sharing into reward systems and culture it won't change.

If you ask a question in a company – can you help me with this? – you need to know that it is alright to ask such questions, have a reasonable expectation that you will get an answer, and be able to find the best person to approach. Before they answer, the person questioned also has a number of barriers. Who is the person asking the question? Will they try to take credit for the answer? Will I get into trouble if I answer?

There are a lot of sociological and psychological issues that organizations need to get at before knowledge starts flowing around. You can do all you like with technology but issues like politics, permission and power are extraordinarily important.

So organizations need to change for intellectual capital to be valued and to create value?

Radical changes in the structure of organizations are required. The law and economic theory say that a company is a bundle of assets. Information Age fact says it is really a beehive of ideas. That change has profound implications for how companies are set up and run – and how they compete.

Companies exist to provide purpose, to be a magnet for intellectual capital, to host conversations and house tacit knowledge, to offer a warranty in terms of brand and reputation, and to perform financial and administrative services.

Are organizations changing?

The best companies in every industry have begun the process of identifying themselves with their ideas more than with their assets. Companies now share assets through outsourcing. Cisco owns less than a handful of factories that actually make products. Most of its products are not touched by Cisco people. There are more and more joint ventures and alliances, odd hybrid structures, professional service firms going public to gain access to capital markets. There are all kinds of blurring of what were once fairly clear boundaries between one company and the next.

Already intellectual capital is being measured at national level. Is this helpful?

We know that knowledge is created when smart people talk to each other. Clusters are intense places of interaction. Governments can encourage that by looking at taxation and immigration to see what they can do to attract the brightest people in the world. Human brains have always been randomly distributed.

There are a profusion of models and measures of intellectual capital. Will there be one dominant and accepted measure?

There is no sense that there will ever be one measure but every company needs to be measuring in some way what its knowledge assets are and how well it is investing in them and exploiting them.

There are some people who see knowledge as packaged goods. They want to know where to sign up to get some of that. They finish with cans of soup and no can openers. The right approach is not packaged goods but to start with an understanding of what is the knowledge that matters. You don't have to have the same knowledge or knowledge assets as anyone else. If you do, you're not unique.

How would you describe the process by which intellectual capital can be managed?

First, you need to identify and evaluate the role of knowledge in your business – as input, process and output. How knowledge intensive is the business? Who gets paid for what knowledge? Who pays? How much? Does whoever owns the knowledge also create the most value?

Second, match the revenues you've just found with the knowledge assets that produce them. What are the expertise, capabilities, brands, intellectual properties, processes and other intellectual capital that create value for you? What is the mixture of human capital, structural capital and customer capital assets?

Third, develop a strategy for investing in and exploiting your intellectual assets. What is your value proposition, source of control and profit model? What strategies exist to increase the knowledge intensity of your business? In what ways can you increase your ability to leverage your intellectual assets? Can you improve results by restructuring intellectual assets (for example, converting human capital into structural capital or vice versa)?

Finally, improve the efficiency of knowledge work and knowledge workers. Bearing in mind that knowledge work does not necessarily follow the linear path that physical labour often does, how can you increase knowledge workers' productivity?

Section 4

STRATEGIC WISDOM

To many in the business world, strategy formulation remains the pinnacle of corporate endeavour. But as business becomes ever faster, strategy appears increasingly disconnected from events. What use is strategy in a business world where the rules of the game are being reinvented on a daily basis?

The arrival of the Internet threw strategic plans up in the air. The strategic preoccupations of just a few years ago were abandoned in the scramble to take businesses online. (Companies may have talked about e-business strategies, but most were forced to make it up as they went along.) That's the trouble with strategy: while the CEO is busy staring at the big picture, the canvas has a nasty habit of unravelling.

Ricardo Semler is one of the few prepared to admit it. Semler's 1993 book *Maverick* launched his career on the international speaking circuit. In it he shared his experiences of worker participation at his Brazilian manufacturing company Semco. Most recently the company has expanded the business from manufacturing to Internet services.

In the early 1990s, Semco employees were selling cooling towers for large commercial buildings. When customers lamented the high cost of maintaining the towers, the salespeople saw an opportunity to launch a new business. This became a $30 million property maintenance business, and led to the creation of an online exchange for the management of commercial construction projects. Yet Semler is frank about how this success was achieved without recourse to a strategy: 'We never planned to go digital, but we're going digital nonetheless.'

This should concern the strategy industry, especially the traditional consulting firms. The strategy powerhouses such as McKinsey & Company, the Boston Consulting Group, Bain & Co. built multi-million dollar businesses from doing clients' strategic thinking for them. The Internet seemed to catch them napping. They trailed along in its wake and only recently have begun to reassert themselves. When strategy is your business this is not a good sign.

For the strategy industry, however, the current concerns are just the latest setback in a long and often chequered career. In 1965, Igor Ansoff published the first book specifically devoted to the topic. It was called, appropriately enough, *Corporate Strategy*. For the first time, it recognized the role of strategic decision-making by senior management as an explicit activity. Strategy was born.

The 1960s and 1970s were a golden age for business strategists. Regiments of bright young graduates were paid large salaries to sit in corporate strategic planning departments removed from the cut and thrust of day-to-day operations and gaze into the future.

But then in the 1980s it all seemed to go wrong. One after another, the strategists in a string of seemingly unassailable companies were wrong-footed by new competition. Strategic planning departments were dismantled. Strategy looked to be in trouble. But into the breach stepped Harvard's Michael Porter, with his Five Forces framework. Porter's model provided a wider view of competitive pressures and opportunities and quickly became the new strategists' bible.

By the early 1990s, however, strategy was back on the ropes. In many companies, strategists had been replaced by downsizers. In his 1994 book, *The Rise and Fall of Strategic Planning*, Professor Henry Mintzberg seemed to sound the death knell of the professional strategist. Strategy, he said, cannot be planned but must emerge by 'synthesis' from changes taking place inside and outside the company.

Then, once again, new thinking reinvigorated the discipline. 1994 also saw the publication of *Competing for the Future*, the book which established the term 'core competencies' in the business lexicon. Gary Hamel and CK Prahalad's tome helped redefine how companies thought about strategy.

Today, the established strategy thinkers are having to make way for a crop of newcomers. Porter's Five Forces framework may still be required reading for MBA students and consultants, but an outpouring of books and articles is reinventing strategy for the twenty-first century. The name of the new game is to develop strategies that redefine the rules. Strategy is reinventing itself.

GARY HAMEL: THE RADICAL FRINGE

Gary Hamel has been labelled 'the world's reigning strategy guru' and 'the most influential thinker on strategy in the Western world'. He calls for radical innovation in business, telling companies that they must continually reinvent themselves, not just at times of crisis. His landmark book, co-authored with C K Prahalad, Competing for the Future, *was BusinessWeek's book of the year in 1995. Its 2000 sequel,* Leading the Revolution, *was also a bestseller.*

Hamel is a founder of Strategos, an international consulting firm, director of the Woodside Institute, a non-profit research organization, and a visiting professor at London Business School.

Gary Hamel talked from his office in Woodside, California.

What is the basis of your latest thinking?

The basic proposition of my recent work is that most of the things which moved earnings and share prices upwards during the last decade have reached their arithmetic limit.

One hundred years from now, people will look back at the last decade, especially the last half of the decade, as an economic aberration. It was a time when a variety of forces conspired together positively to create a buoyant economic climate.

First, there was huge growth in technology and IT spending. Go back to 1990 and US companies invested about 19% of their capital expenditure on technology. By 2000 they were spending 59%. Capital spending tripled. It was the longest capital spending boom in history. That fuelled the share prices of IBM, Cisco and Sun and everyone else in the technology sector. That's not going to happen again. Capital spending is not going to triple over the next decade.

The second positive force was an unprecedented attack on inefficiency. Over the last decade we have seen re-engineering, restructuring, downsizing, enterprise resource planning and customer relationship management. All of these things, whatever their names, were essentially concerned with doing more with less. There's a lot of data which says that companies now have reached the point of diminishing returns in their efficiency programs. They are having to work harder and harder.

The third thing was an orgy of mergers and acquisitions (M&As). In 1990 there was roughly $600 billion worth of global M&As. There were $3.5 trillion by the end of the decade. If M&As had continued to grow at that pace there would have been one company left in the US.

It was possible for executives to rely on a rising economic tide on which to float their boat. The tide is now receding. There is no evidence that somehow substantial economic expansion is going to rescue the day.

So you take a pessimistic view on the prospects for economic growth?

I am not pessimistic on growth overall, but right now most companies don't have any strategy which goes beyond retrenchment. Suddenly, timidity is in fashion once again. Retrenchment doesn't buy you growth, it doesn't buy you a future. At best it buys you time.

There is enormous enthusiasm for moving back to basics. You can't argue with that at one level. Of course, you need to focus on the basics. The dilemma is most companies don't have a lot of options. Most companies, for example, can't grow revenues by selling the same things in the same old way to the same customers.

One of the huge blind spots for a lot of managers is that they've forgotten that productivity has two elements – the efficiency with which you use your inputs, your labour and your capital, and the value placed on your output. Executives know a lot about the efficiency side of the equation but not about their output.

Despite all the consolidation in the global car industry over recent years, the most profitable car makers are BMW and Porsche, and they are couple of the smallest. They may not have the global purchasing efficiencies of GM or Ford, but they create things people love.

On the cost side, most companies have reached the point of diminishing returns. But if you look at companies which are doing best in difficult times, companies like Dell, Wal-Mart, Jet Blue, and Ryanair, all brought radical innovation to the cost structure. Their costs are not five or ten per cent lower but fifty or eighty per cent.

Are you saying that retrenchment simply won't lead to growth?

My argument is that the more difficult the economic times, the more one is tempted to retrench, the more radical innovation becomes the only way forwards. In a discontinuous world, only radical innovation will create new wealth.

At one level, executives are getting that message. They know that they can't do the same things. But there is a huge gap between the rhetoric and the reality.

CEOs will say that they need to innovate and put innovation as one of their top two or three priorities. But if you go down a few levels in the organization and talk to mid-level employees, you should ask have you been trained in innovation? What is the process you plug into if you have a new idea? How quickly can you locate talent to push ideas forward? Ask these questions and it's obvious that most companies have not institutionalized innovation in a meaningful way. Innovation is a ghetto. It is seen as something for a few people in product development, R&D, or the corporate business development function. It is not seen as the responsibility of every single employee every single day. Most companies haven't even begun to either unleash or monetize the imagination that exists.

It is the same situation as we had around 1970 in terms of quality. People knew that quality was important but didn't know the processes or systems which could enable this to happen. All the processes and systems – pareto analysis, quality circles and so on – later known as total quality management, were being built at the time. Executives in the West had very little knowledge of them and didn't know what to do.

The question I have been asking is how do you do for innovation what W Edwards Deming and others did for quality?

What is the pay-off from better understanding innovation?

Innovation drives wealth creation. There's no other conclusion you can reach.

A product advantage can come and go but if you commit early to building a complex and deeply embedded capability, it is very difficult to catch up. Companies that commit themselves to innovation – like Whirlpool, Cemex, Shell and a few others – are going to have a profound advantage. It might not be evident right away but once you get a lead it is difficult for others to catch up. Over the last 40 years, Western car makers haven't recaptured even a single point of market share from their Japanese competitors. The Western car industry has continued to lose market share.

How can companies develop the capability to innovate?

Making innovation a real capability requires not an overlay of a few small adjustments, it requires a fundamental rethink of your most basic business principles. Today, the goal of becoming incrementally better is engrained in our thinking, in our language, in our reward mechanisms and everything we do. Innovation is seen as an exceptional thing which happens once in a while, almost by accident, on the fringe. To change that is not easy.

Think of the legacy of the industrial age – hierarchy, control, replication, quality. These are hugely important but in many ways they are toxic to the process of innovation and creativity, experimentation, imagination, self-organization.

We haven't really challenged the primacy of optimization and incremental improvement. Fundamentally, innovation can't be at the edge. Innovation has to be central to the purpose of organizations. We have to systematically train people in new ways of thinking. We have to create new metrics. Most of the metrics companies use – ROI, EVA, and so on – push us into thinking simply about incremental improvements. We still have a very deep belief in management processes, which are the antithesis of innovation.

One of them is that alignment is always a virtue – everyone reading from the same page, all the wood behind the arrow, whatever metaphor you use. Perfect alignment is death.

In a world of enormous change, the scope for experimentation inside your company has to match the scope for experimentation outside. We have to re-engineer management processes to minimize the time between an idea and wealth creation. It's not the supply chain that needs shortening and automating, it's the innovation chain that needs shortening and automating.

What needs to happen now?

Companies shouldn't mistake what happened in the 1990s as real innovation. The 1990s were a product of the dealmakers and the dream merchants.

Three principles are the foundation for trying to move forward. First, radical innovation: in an increasingly non-linear world, only non-linear ideas create wealth. Innovation is the only insurance against irrelevance. Second, requisite variety. Is there scope for experimentation within the company? Is there a willingness to make mistakes? Most organizations have way too little strategic experimentation. Third, resource attraction, which is different from resource allocation. We need to learn from markets. Markets outperform hierarchies every time. Most organizations today look a whole lot more like the Soviet Union than we would like to admit.

COSTAS MARKIDES: ESCAPING THE JUNGLE

Incessant change, relentless competition, bright young upstarts stealing hard-won market share, the deluge of data, a constant demand for innovation, not to mention the vicissitudes of the world economy, all make for a turbulent and uncertain business environment. So, who needs a strategy when mere survival from one day to the next is the top priority?

Much of the current crop of strategic thinking comes from outside the US. In Europe, IMD's Paul Strebel calls on companies to practice 'high speed strategy'. Other commentators point to new strategic imperatives. W Chan Kim and Renée Mauborgne of INSEAD advocate a switch from thinking about strategy in terms of existing competitors to thinking in terms of creating entirely new markets, or redefining existing markets.

Strategy is reinventing itself and among those leading the way is Costas Markides. Markides is Robert P Bauman Professor of Strategic Leadership at London Business School. His books include Strategic Management for the Next Economy *(with Michael Cusumano) and* All the Right Moves: A Guide to Crafting Breakthrough Strategy.

You were recently described by the Wall Street Journal as being the creator of something called 'jungle strategy'. Do you plead guilty?

I was asked whether a company really needs a strategy in today's turbulent and uncertain times. My reply was: imagine you find yourself in the middle of a dark and hostile jungle. If you want to get out of the jungle, do you need a strategy?

Think about it. In the dense foliage, you cannot see beyond a few feet. You want to get out of this jungle but you don't know how and you don't know which way to turn. There is total uncertainty. How then can you get out alive? Well, the last thing you want to do is to stay still, paralysed by uncertainty. You need to analyse your position based on the available information and then decide on a direction. That's the first principle of strategy – the need to make difficult choices based on what information you have at the time. You take stock, gather information based on that and then start walking. The worst thing is to stay still. That's the second principle of strategy – the need to stop analysing and start doing, even if you are not entirely sure that what you are doing is going to turn out to be the right thing.

After you start walking, new information comes your way. The new information may allow you to revise your original direction. That's the third principle of strategy – the need to learn as you go along and modify your strategy through trial and error. If you meet a wild animal or run into a canyon, your strategy (or direction) has to change. Therefore, strategy is all about making difficult choices in the face of uncertainty and then learning as you go along and adjusting your original choices. When you think of it like this, it's obvious that you need a strategy even (or especially) when there is a lot of uncertainty out there! You need a sense of direction otherwise you are a rudderless boat being torn apart by the waves.

But you also need a strategy that is different from the competition.

Exactly right! The question, of course, is how to come up with a differentiated strategy. I recently talked to a group of CEOs from the same industry. One asked how they could be expected to have different strategies when they all had the same suppliers, were structured in much the same ways, received their information from the same sources, used the same consultants and so on.

In reply I referred to an exercise I use in my classes. I ask the students to see how many times they can arm wrestle with their neighbour in 30 seconds. So, the students set themselves up in pairs and begin to arm wrestle. Most of them compete and succeed in pushing their colleagues' arms down a few times, at best. But there's always a pair who agree to co-operate and press their arms up and down dozens of times in 30 seconds.

The strategy of being different wins! But how did these students come up with such a different approach from everybody else? The people in the classroom all receive the same information from me; identical instructions. The difference lies in mental processing; how the information given is processed. The same applies to companies. How you process the information around you will determine what you do.

Indeed, this is what differentiates innovators from other companies. Most companies try to become better than their competitors. But, for almost all companies other than the established leader, being better is not the right way. They need to play a different game. Look at EasyJet, e*trade or Schwab. They are companies not intent on being better but on playing a different game. They thought of new ways of playing the game. The managers of these companies face the same information as everyone else in their industries, yet they process this information differently and come up with differentiated strategies. Companies get the same inputs, but it's what they do with the inputs to change the rules of the game that matters.

Should an established company try to play a different game?

Many established companies develop a winning strategy and then spend all their time trying to improve it and make it better. They rarely consider 'cannibalizing' their current strategy in favour of a 'different' one. They find the risks for doing so too high. Yet, all around us, established companies are being toppled by newcomers that adopt different strategies. My personal belief is that companies must continue to improve their existing strategy but they must also continuously strive to discover new or different strategies. They should try to be better and different at the same time.

The question is, how can a company play two games simultaneously? Michael Porter suggests that doing this is so difficult that most companies that attempt it will fail. His advice is for companies to focus on only one game. His Harvard colleague, Clay Christensen, suggests that a company can play two games at the same time but the new game needs to be separate from the main business.

My own research suggests that although doing so is difficult, companies can still play two games without necessarily separating them. More importantly, my research suggests that when established companies are attacked by a new way of playing the game, they do not necessarily have to respond to it by adopting the new game. Look at what happened with Gillette back in the 1970s when it came under attack by Bic. The game adopted by Bic was certainly different from Gillette's game. But Gillette did not respond by adopting the Bic game. Instead, it invested $1 billion in its existing game to develop a superior product – the Mach 3 – which was then used to 'destroy' Bic and the disposable razor threat. Who buys disposable razors now?

What established companies need to appreciate is that the new disruptive ways of playing the game are not God-sent. The new ways are not preordained to win out. Established companies could respond by 'killing off' the new ways. For example, why is Internet banking the game of the future? Is it more convenient or more efficient than traditional banking? Why don't banks respond to it, *not* by adopting it, but by making their traditional operations so good that no consumer in their right minds would find banking over the Internet an attractive proposition?

Consider also the case of Swatch. In the 1970s, the Swiss watchmakers competed on the basis of their craftsmanship. Then, Japanese companies (like Seiko) attacked by offering better prices, the latest technology, and more features. Everybody thought that this would be the end of the Swiss watch industry – then Swatch arrived! Instead of taking it on the chin, Swatch hit back at the Japanese. But instead of trying to compete with them on their terms (i.e. price and features), Swatch introduced a new competitive dimension – style and design – as the basis for competition.

Consider Merrill Lynch today. It competes on the basis of research and advice. Schwab and e*trade have now attacked it on the basis of cheaper transaction costs and faster execution of trades. Merrill Lynch will not succeed against them if it too chooses to play the price and speed game. You cannot out-Xerox Xerox! What they have to do is innovate and discover new competitive dimensions – different reasons as to why a customer should buy from them.

What are the differences between what you are saying and the arguments of the likes of Gary Hamel or Chan Kim?

We're speaking about the same things and use many of the same examples. But we all try to differentiate ourselves by using different words! Seriously, though, I'd like to think that what I am saying could be differentiated from others' research on two fronts.

First, I'd like to differentiate between innovation and creativity (or invention). Coming up with new ideas is not innovation – it's creativity. Innovation is deciding which ideas to pick on and implement to create value. A lot of research out there tends to emphasize creativity rather than innovation. For example, other academics have written about making strategy democratic so that everyone in a company could contribute strategic ideas. They have also written about the need of 'bringing Silicon Valley or capitalism inside' the organization. This is all good stuff but the end result is improved creativity, not innovation.

Innovation is much more than this. It is about coming up with ideas and then finding ways to scale them up so as to create mass markets out of them. For example, consider the market for PCs. Who is the 'innovator' in this market? Most people think that the answer is Apple or, perhaps, Osborne. But who really created the mass market for PCs? Who is to be credited with the fact that the personal computer is not some high-tech gimmick that only nerds use but is instead a fixture in every home? The answer is simple – IBM. They scaled it up. They created the mass market. Yet, nobody considers IBM as an innovator.

Therefore, innovation is not just coming up with ideas but also scaling them up to create big markets. Most of the dot-coms failed because they didn't know how to sell to customers, to bring ideas to a mass market. The question for Amazon.com, therefore, is whether they will convert Internet bookselling into a mass market. I bet it won't be Amazon that does this. My money goes to Wal-Mart to do this.

The trouble is that while coming up with ideas is celebrated as innovative, the act of scaling them up into big markets is not! Even worse, scaling up rather than coming up with new ideas is what big companies are good at. Unfortunately, they often forget this and try instead to become brilliantly creative like the small start-up firms. Instead of taking the ideas of others and converting them into big markets, they focus on coming up with ideas themselves. Unfortunately, this is what small firms excel at.

Over the last ten years we have tried to convert big firms into small firms. There is a lot of talk about injecting big corporations with the entrepreneurial culture of the small firm, or breaking up the big ones to make them as agile and flexible as the small ones. This is like trying to help a 70-year-old win the 100 metres at the Olympics! It won't happen. The big firm will never become as creative as the small firm. What the big corporation is good at is 'scaling up', not creativity. Our attention should shift towards making the big corporation better at what it is good at – not making it like the small ones.

There is a cultural bias in favour of coming up with ideas and a real lack of appreciation for the challenging task of taking the idea and converting it into a mass market. Similarly, there is a bias in defining innovation as something new. But the real trick is how to convert something new from being a plaything of the few into the mass market.

What's the second area that differentiates your work on strategic innovation?

If you ask a group of CEOs how to make their organizations more innovative, you will get a huge laundry list of ideas on how to do it

– allow experiments, reward new ideas, do not punish mistakes, and so on. The problem is not that they don't know how to do it but that it doesn't happen.

So, why don't they do it? Senior executives know what they can do to promote innovation. But the personal risks are simply too high. Innovation carries a huge personal risk so how many people would actually do it? Not to mention that at the end of the year, what they get evaluated on is not innovative ideas, but delivering the numbers.

But over and above this, what we forget is that innovation is an art. Even if you have all the ingredients, it does not mean that we will get innovation. The key is how you put it all together. The baking of the cake is more important than the actual ingredients. That's where business schools go wrong. We give students ingredients. We teach people tools but not the art of actually baking the cake. That is an art which requires practice, common sense and experimentation to develop.

So, what needs to change?

We need to train people *how* to think, not what to think. We also need to give people a sense that organizations are not there simply to make money for individuals and the company, but that they have a social purpose in life. The important thing is for young people to get into business not only because it's a good way to make money, but also because through their companies, they can help create something that improves the state of the world.

For example, the young people that worked as a team to develop the Apple Mac were not just making a computer. They were on a mission to change the way people thought about computers. In the end, galvanizing people isn't about money but about having a purpose beyond money. Making money is implicit.

You have talked of the 'moral' corporation. What do you mean by this?

The modern corporation is very delicate. It must be able to make an accurate assessment of the external environment so it takes the right strategic position. In addition, it must also remain true to the unwritten moral contract with employees. This contract promises to provide employees with an environment that sustains then and allows them to grow as individuals.

To achieve this delicate balancing act we require corporations which have different structures, processes, mindsets and behaviours than has been the norm for the last 50 years. We need to totally rethink how we manage corporations.

If they are to be flexible and fluid, companies need to become amoeba-like – able to move one way while always responding to local stimuli and changing direction in response to new information from the environment.

We're back in the jungle again?

Yes. And this can only be achieved by giving people autonomy and the freedom to monitor what's going on around them and respond as they see fit.

Isn't this a recipe for chaos?

Not if we have organizations with strong values and beliefs which act as the parameters within which people are free to operate. That's the moral corporation.

JAMES CHAMPY: WHAT RE-ENGINEERING DID NEXT

Today, James Champy is chairman of the Perot System's consulting practice.

But he is best known as one of the chief architects of the re-engineering movement of the 1990s. Re-engineering the Corporation, *the 1993 book he co-authored with Michael Hammer, was on the* New York Times *bestseller list for more than a year. It sold over two million copies and catapulted Champy to international guru status.*

Champy and Hammer described their book as a 'manifesto for a business revolution'. It established re-engineering as the big business idea of the early 1990s, creating a whole new consulting industry. The message of re-engineering was that organizations needed to identify their key processes and re-engineer them to make them as efficient as possible. Peripheral processes, and by implication, peripheral employees, were to be stripped away. 'Don't automate; obliterate,' Hammer proclaimed, coining what many came to regard as the re-engineering mantra.

A wave of downsizing followed as corporations throughout the world obliterated in the name of re-engineering. As the human cost of job cuts became apparent, it created a backlash. Champy's 1995 follow-up book, Re-engineering Management, *argued that management, too, required drastic medicine. But managers were unwilling to inflict it upon themselves. The re-engineering revolution stalled. Champy, however, remains committed to the cause.*

His recent book, X-Engineering the Corporation, *argues that managers must now look beyond re-engineering and cross (as in X) boundaries they've never crossed before. The walls between a company, its customers and its suppliers – and even between competitors – are falling, he argues. The advent of the Internet makes it possible to redesign processes across organizational borders.*

James Champy talks about what the re-engineering revolution achieved, how it was hijacked by corporate downsizers, and why X-engineering is the next big thing.

Was the re-engineering revolution of the 1990s a success or a failure?

I believe it was a success. I also believe that it's a revolution that is by no means over. We positioned these as revolutionary ideas but I think the revolution is still in progress. It is still ongoing. I have no doubt that it will eventually be seen as a success, but the truth is it's a long struggle.

Today many managers associate re-engineering with downsizing. Do you regret that?

No. Not in any personal sense. The only regret I have is that some managers will have closed their minds to re-engineering. That's a big problem – not for me, but for them and their businesses. I feel regretful that the term switches people off. But I have not given up making the case. The time has come to make it in a more powerful way.

Are there things that you wished you'd done differently? Should you have given more attention to the people issues, for example?

We possibly could have been more prescriptive. We could have laid out more in terms of method and technique. The truth is that a lot of other people did that. If you look at the consultancies that grew in the 1990s, most of them – all of them in fact – grew around re-engineering or process work.

But to your question about whether we could have been more conscious of the people issue, I think the organizational issues represent a fundamental challenge in any major process of corporate change – and always will be. Always. The real challenge here is that we and the other practitioners – and even the organizational behaviourists – have not discovered anything new about how to change corporate behaviour or human behaviour in the last fifty years, never mind the last ten years.

What's striking is that I can redesign a business process in a matter of days but it still takes years to implement. Peter Drucker argued that corporate culture change – corporate behaviour change – was about as difficult to make as changing the culture of a country. I always wanted to think that it was much more doable. But I now believe that the change cycles around process and how we do business should be measured in decades, not months or single years.

Can a company's culture be re-engineered?

I think that culture can be re-engineered but it's a five to ten year process. If there was any failure with re-engineering I think it was the failure to recognize that these process changes take place within a larger corporate culture – and that does take years to change.

Your latest work is around X-engineering – what is it and why is it important now?

It's extending the process redesign across corporate boundaries. Although most companies have not completed the re-engineering they need to do, the next major opportunity for significantly improving the performance of a business or an industry is to look at the collaborative redesign of processes. And it isn't just at the interface. So it isn't just saying my sales process doesn't match the way you buy; it's really going much deeper. It involves understanding how a company operates and how its customers operate and what the processes might look like if they were fundamentally redesigned.

If you look at a paper-based transaction for many large companies, it will cost a few hundred dollars to do that transaction; if you look at a telephone-based transaction then maybe 10 or 20 dollars. But if you look at a so-called digitized transaction – an Internet based transaction – it costs cents. So you're going from hundreds of dollars to tens of dollars to a matter of cents to do a transaction. If you look right across the supply chain, there could be extraordinary cost savings – 30 to 40 per cent is not an unreasonable figure – both for the seller and the buyer.

People have been talking about virtual and boundary-less organizations for a while now, but organizations don't seem to have changed that much?

You're right, the notion of the boundary-less or connected organization has been around for a while, but it remains a notion. The enabler is the Internet. And it is the Internet that will allow the eventual cross boundary prophecy to become real in the next generation.

The other issue is the depth of the change. This is about a very deep form of collaboration with your suppliers and your customers. The underlying theories in this work are really in harmonization, standardization, and transparency. Those ideas are not easily accepted by companies. This work is going to be very hard to do.

Let's just take transparency. Most companies operate on the assumption that they have proprietary information to protect – that what they do is in some way proprietary – where the truth is that 95 per cent of what they do is exactly what their competitors to do. If you look at their processes, they are the same as their competitors.

Now that's a hard notion for managers to accept. But the notion of a boundary-less organization requires transparency – a willingness to be open, to lay out all your processes except those that are truly your distinctive processes.

Which companies are good at X-engineering?

Some of the companies that are doing this well are the ones who have the advantage of starting their process design from scratch. Dell and Cisco Systems are probably quintessential X-engineers. Michael Dell started with a lot of these principles – like build-to-order – which was his customer-focused approach, and if you look at the way he's extended that back into the supply chain, he has built a masterful supply chain that is highly integrated operationally with his suppliers.

Cisco is the same, especially on the customer facing side. So these are companies that started with principles of transparency, of harmonization, and of standardization and were able to make it work.

A truly collaborative community or network implies far closer interdependencies. But how do you allocate benefits between the different members?

That's a very important question. And the answer is that it won't work unless you divide up the benefits. Everyone has to enter the conversation recognizing that one of the principal drivers is that there have to be financial benefits for everyone. Otherwise everyone isn't going to play.

One of the problems with re-engineering, and one of the reasons there is some edge to it or anger or upset, is that the chief beneficiaries were the shareholders. The efficiencies occurred on the back of workers – because real re-engineering wasn't done; all that happened was downsizing. You got half the workers doing twice the amount of work, and you got customers who actually got poorer, not better, service. Costs were reduced and the shareholder benefited – that's all.

Does X-engineering apply to companies in Brazil and India as much as firms in the US and Western Europe?

In time they will have to adopt X-engineering because what is fundamentally going on in many of those countries is the outsourcing of work in process. And the company that will succeed and build scale in those countries will have learned how to do X-engineering extremely well.

Re-engineering gave rise to a huge consulting industry. Is X-engineering another consulting product or can companies do it themselves?

I believe that companies will always need some amount of advice. But I think this is actually something companies need to do more on their own. X-engineering fundamentally affects the strategy of the business. It requires you to rethink what the business proposition is – and is there a business proposition that goes beyond simply being a low-price producer? We are in a period of great product commoditization. Everybody is feeling under cost pressure. But nobody wants to be just competing on price forever – that can be a deadly spiral. So I think companies are being challenged with thinking about what a new business proposition might look like. And that's hard work. No consultant who breezes through your business can help you with that. You have to really understand the needs of your customers in the marketplace.

Companies are increasingly seen not as machines but as communities of people. The onus is on relationships rather than processes. How do you reconcile that with your theories?

You must have both. There must be trust in relationships. X-engineering in particular requires trusting relationships. Companies know that we're in this with our customers and suppliers to benefit everybody in that network. There has to be trust and there have to be relationships that allow for collaborative design.

W CHAN KIM AND RENÉE MAUBORGNE: STRATEGIC MOVES

Modern thinking on strategy is divided between those who think that the basic building block is a company's competencies, and those who think that industries rather than companies are the basic element. W Chan Kim and Renée Mauborgne think differently.

Kim and Mauborgne are based at INSEAD, the leading European business school situated in the forest of Fontainebleau, just south of Paris. Kim is the Boston Consulting Group Bruce D. Henderson Chair Professor of International Management, and Mauborgne, the INSEAD Distinguished Fellow and Affiliate Professor of Strategy and Management. Their reputation is built around a series of acclaimed articles in the Harvard Business Review *and is supported by a substantial database stretching all the way back to 1850.*

According to Kim and Mauborgne, the basic element of strategy is not an industry nor a company, but what they call 'smart strategic moves'. Talking at INSEAD, they explain more about their challenge to the strategic orthodoxy.

You are critical of the language used in discussing business strategy.

Mauborgne: The essence of business strategy can be traced to military strategy. That's why traditionally the field of strategy talked about headquarters rather than head office. In terrain and war, there's only so much land that exists. Fundamentally, that explains why business strategy – including competitive strategy – has been predominantly based on how you divide up an existing pie. It's about relative power. It's a zero sum game because you cannot multiply the size of land available.

The question is: why has the field of business strategy, sometimes implicitly, sometimes explicitly, taken this assumption to be true? While strategy in war may be limited to dividing up existing non-changeable land masses, if there is one lesson the world has taught us over the last hundred years it is that in the realm of business, the new market spaces that can be created are infinite. What you see if you look historically is that real gains came when people created an entirely new area – a whole new market space. You can create a win–win game. You can create new land. Just think of the number of industries that exist today that did not exist even thirty years prior. Scientifically, we know that the amount of chemical compounds that exist has not changed over time. But look at what you had in the beginning – just dinosaurs. And today, by creatively combining them in numerous new ways we have … Starbucks. What we can buy today in a Seven Eleven store beats what a king like Louis XIV had. The possibilities are endless.

How does such profusion link to your research?

Kim: We looked back at 150 years of data and found that the pace of industry creation has speeded up. We asked which industries were around in 1900 and are still around today? And it turns out that apart from the basic industries such as cars and steel, almost nothing. Look back to the major industries of 1970 and very few, if any, are now significant. The big growth industries in the past thirty years have been the computer industry, software, gas-fired electricity plants, cell phones, and the café bar concept for starters. But in 1970, not one of those industries existed in a meaningful way, and that's just thirty years back. The pattern continues as you dig into the past. The big industries of 1940 aren't those of 1910, and so on. We have a hugely underestimated capacity to create new industries. Everyone assumes that the number of industries stays the same over time, but it doesn't. And if this is where the bulk of wealth has been created, shouldn't the field of strategy systematically explore and understand the path to new market space creation?

The next question we asked was how come some companies rise and fall? The companies featured in *In Search of Excellence* struggled afterwards. Then along comes another bestseller, *Built to Last*, that says the trouble was that a long enough time frame was not considered. Then *Creative Destruction* comes out and says if you take out the industry effects, some of these companies are even underperforming.

Our conclusion is that companies are the wrong unit of analysis. So are industries. Any company is excellent at certain points in time. It depends on the leaders and managers. There's no such thing as a permanently great company, nor a permanently great industry. But there are permanently great strategic moves. And the strategic move that we found matters centrally is the creation and capturing of new market space.

What do you mean by a strategic move?

Mauborgne: By *strategic move* we mean the actions of players in conceiving, launching, and realizing their business ideas. In each strategic move, there are winners, losers, and mere survivors.

Can you give me an example?

Mauborgne: A snapshot of the auto-industry from 1900 to 1940 is instructive. Ford's Model T, launched in 1908, triggered the industry's growth and profitability, replacing the horse drawn carriage with the car for American households. It lifted Ford's market share from 9 to 60 per cent.

The Model T was the strategic move that ignited the automotive industry. But in 1924, it was overtaken by another move, this time by GM. Contrary to Ford's functional one-colour one-car single model strategy, GM created the new market space of emotional stylized cars with 'a car for every purpose and purse'. Not only was the auto industry's growth and profitability again catapulted to new heights, but GM's market share jumped from 20 to 50 per cent while Ford's fell from 60 to 20 per cent.

So, understanding the context and the right strategic moves is the key to success. There will always be a debate about rising and falling companies and industries. What the Body Shop did was absolutely brilliant. It created a new market space in a highly competitive industry. The problem was that they didn't realize what made it a brilliant strategic move, and when everyone imitated them they needed to do it again.

Isn't this just industry lifecycle?

Kim: There doesn't have to be an industry lifecycle. Because people say there is an industry lifecycle, we accept it. Look at Cemex, the world's third largest cement producer from Mexico. It is challenging the industry lifecycle by creating cement as an emotional product – which is also helping to address the country's housing issues. In Mexico, it usually takes about 8–10 years to build a house and you build it room by room. The issue is that whenever people have any cash, they are always spending it on weddings or other ceremonies or on jewellery or other expensive gifts. So Cemex has turned cement into an emotional product by saying if you really love somebody, give them cement. Give them a room to build because you are giving them a house, a room, you are giving them a home. They'll have love and laughter. And they have totally re-branded cement as the best gift you can give someone because you are giving them a home. This has taken a flat industry to higher profit margins and turned it into a growth industry. Similarly, the coffee industry was dead until Starbucks came along.

The moment you take an industry deterministic view of your company, you are a victim of that industry. The moment you sit back and say, 'how can we create a whole new industry', then you start to break that cycle. All industries are created not by big resources but by big ideas.

You also talk about 'fair process'. What does this mean?

Mauborgne: Value innovation is about strategy; fair process is about management. Transformation requires that companies earn the intellectual and emotional commitment of their employees. To do so requires a degree of fairness in making and executing decisions. All a company's plans will come to nothing if they are not supported by employees. Fair process is based on the simple human need for intellectual and emotional recognition. Without fair process it can be difficult for companies even to achieve something their people generally support.

What are the basic questions companies need to ask themselves if they are to embrace fair process?

Kim: First, they need to ask whether they engage people in decisions that affect them. Fair process is about engagement. Do they ask for input and allow people to refute the merit of one another's ideas? Do they explain why decisions are made and why some opinions have been overridden? And, after a decision is made, are the rules clearly stated so that people understand the new standards, the targets, responsibilities and penalties? Building trust was the big issue at Davos this year.

But isn't fair process idealistic? In the real world, fairness is inevitably compromised.

Kim: There is a difference between a fair process and a fair outcome. Power – money, resources and structural power – is all about outcome-driven measures. The minute you have the power and the resources, often process takes a distant back seat. Fair process is seen as a nuisance. That is when companies often do not act on the insight that people are their most valuable asset. The issue is that when companies do that, they are failing to leverage the voluntary cooperation and idea sharing of their people. It doesn't matter if you work in a profit or non-profit organization, fair process is a motivational tool which is critically important. But many companies overlook this and focus overridingly on outcomes.

In the knowledge economy, where idea sharing is even more critical, fair process also becomes more important. Ideas cannot be supervised so easily. There is a need for voluntary co-operation, willingness to go beyond the call of duty has to come from the heart. Our research has found fair process to generate voluntary co-operation but not outcomes.

What is the cost of the absence of fair process? Look at the missed opportunities in the auto industry alone, where management has repeatedly violated fair process, and labour has vetoed with strikes and sabotage costing tens of billions. A huge management issue of the future will be the opportunities missed.

You see fair process as being of very wide importance?

Mauborgne: Indeed, fair process is central to co-operation, not only in companies but in world peace. Just look at the current lack of support, if not animosity, America is engendering around the world from its once allies. While there was deep sympathy felt around the world after the tragic events of September 11 for America, today America has effectively squandered that good will and even, some might argue, generated a deficit of support around the globe. And why? Trace the process by which the war on Iraq was evolved by the Americans. There was no proper explanation for why Iraq was to be targeted or linked to the events of September 11. Participants at this year's Davos repeatedly asked for sound explanation and proof for the basis of their decisions but feel that this was never provided, hence violating the fair process principle of 'explanation'. America and in particular the US presidency did not engage world leaders in a dialogue on why it was moving down the trajectory that it was. The one-on-one face-to-face dialogues between the US presidency and critical world leaders was dismal, though a war with Iraq would have economic and security implications for them, hence violating the fair process principle of 'engagement'. And lastly, the US presidency did not provide 'expectation clarity', the third fair process principle, to world leaders on what would be expected of them after a fall of Saddam Hussein, in the economic and political recovery of Iraq. It is not surprising that world leaders feel resentment at the US and a violation of intellectual and emotional recognition, and with it goodwill.

HENRY MINTZBERG: SEARCHING FOR BALANCE

Henry Mintzberg is a professional contrarian. He has built a formidable reputation on challenging the corporate orthodoxy. His 1994 book, The Rise and Fall of Strategic Planning, *revealed the sterility of the conventional strategic planning process which had dominated management thinking for years. It confirmed his place as the great debunker of corporate life.*

Mintzberg first came to attention with his 1973 book The Nature of Managerial Work. *Based on his PhD research, it is one of the few (very few) books which examines what managers do rather than discussing what they should do.*

Since then, Mintzberg, a professor at McGill University in Montreal, has applied his heretical attentions to a variety of subjects. In his own field, strategy, he has remained at the forefront of the debate. A champion of strategy as a creative and emergent process, he has consistently defended it against those who seek to reduce it to prescriptive analysis.

Despite his association with business schools, Mintzberg is a long-time critic of the traditional MBA degree. As an alternative, he and colleagues developed the International Masters Program in Practicing Management (IMPM), a global programme which encourages managers to break free of the limitations of functional, and other, perspectives. His book Developing Managers, Not MBAs *questions the usefulness of the classic business school degree.*

Henry Mintzberg talks about the Enron scandal, why MBAs and shareholder value are killing business, and the need to bring balance to the capitalist system.

What does the Enron scandal say to you about the state of management?

Enron is just the most blatantly corrupt example of a lot of legal corruption. You have to question the role of the auditing firms. What's the point of an auditing firm if they don't audit? There are all kinds of things going on in terms of executive compensation and the games being played. It's all being driven by a narrow definition of success that's based on shareholder value. We're out of balance. We're completely obsessed with the economic side of everything.

Would you expect to see more Enrons come to light now?

Companies are covering their backs like mad – even safe companies. Will it come to light after the fact? Yes, I guess more will show. It's not so much the blatantly outrageous acts like Enron; what worries me are the prevailing attitudes in many companies.

It's a form of corruption. It doesn't have to be illegal corruption; it can be a kind of legal corruption: a corruption of values, a corruption of attitude, a corruption of responsibility. The system is sick right down to its roots. Call it shareholder value or whatever, but the obsession with narrow performance and economics skews the way that people think and act. Businesses can't function without some degree of social responsibility.

Is there a role for practising managers in redressing the balance?

Companies have to balance the social with the economic for their own good as well as for society's good. But even CEOs are just cogs in the machine. How are they going to stand up to a board that sees shareholder value as the only important dimension? Solzhenitsyn said that a society that has no rules like the communist society is abhorrent, but a society that only stays within the letter of the law – he had the United States in mind – is not much better.

Your PhD research in the 1970s studied what managers did. Has that changed much in the intervening years?

No. What has changed is the style of management. As we get more MBAs in companies, so the style of management becomes more disconnected.

What's wrong with MBAs?

Basically, my objection is that MBA programmes claim to be creating managers and they are not.

The MBA is really about business, which would be fine except that people leave these programmes thinking they've been trained to do management. I think every MBA should have a skull and crossbones stamped on their forehead and underneath should be written, 'Warning; not prepared to manage'.

And the issue is not just that they are not trained to manage, but that they are given a totally wrong impression of what managing is;

namely decision-making by analysis. The impression they get from what they've studied is that people skills don't really matter.

So they come out with this distorted view. I've seen it over and over again where people have MBAs and go into managerial positions and don't know what they are doing. So basically, they write reports and plans and do all sorts of information processing things and pretend that it's management. It's killing organizations, and I think it's getting worse over time.

You talk about nuanced management as a better way of managing – what is it and how do you learn it?

I don't think it is a better way of managing, I think it is managing. I think all decent management is nuanced. Bad management is not nuanced; bad management is categorical.

Nuanced management is about getting involved, knowing the business, knowing what's going on day-to-day. For me it's all about getting past all the nonsense that passes for management. It's getting in touch, knowing what's really going on, being responsive – and responsible.

To what extent can and should managers educate themselves – can they apply your techniques on their own?

Largely, managers have to educate themselves because they can't go into educational programmes for very much time. They have to be learning all the time so they have to educate themselves.

You ask about my techniques – I have no techniques. I have ideas, but as soon as they become techniques they start to lose their usefulness. We put a lot of emphasis on reflection – taking time to step back and think about what you can learn from your own experience. I wouldn't call it a technique but it is important. I think managers can learn how to be reflective and then apply it. I think that's what good managers do.

How does your approach to executive education facilitate that?

The way our programmes work is we bring people into a thoughtful atmosphere and we sit them around a table and get them to share their experiences in a low-key way. I'm critical of management programmes that promise boot camps. Managers live boot camps every day of their lives. What they need is to slow down and reflect.

Part of your IMPM programme is delivered in India – why did you choose that country?

We wanted to go to a place that had three things. Number one, a truly developing country – in other words not wealthy but improving. Number two, facility in the English language, and number three, a strong academic infrastructure. India was perfect.

Is managing in India the same as managing anywhere else? Is management universal?

Yes and no. In some ways managing is managing if you describe it in terms of networking and these sorts of things. But on another level, every country has its own approach.

I did a session with some MBA students in Argentina, and I asked the dean of the school if they taught an Argentinean style of management. He said no, they teach the universal style of management. I said you mean the American style. The global style is not global, it is American. The trouble is everywhere else, people think that the universal way of managing is what happens in the United States. But each place has its own different style.

Is the new economy real or just a lot of hype?

There's always a new economy. The automobile industry was part of a new economy too a century ago. So the idea of a new economy is not new. I do think there are new industries that come along. There are some industries undergoing a lot of change and some industries undergoing less change. That's always the case. So it's real – and it's a lot of hype.

At the height of the dot-com frenzy, some people were saying that the old rules of strategy were dead. Where are we now?

I don't think there were ever rules about how to make a strategy and I don't think there are any more. So they can't be dead. I think there were processes that creative people used to put together information and ideas and come up with the direction they should go in. The rules should always have been bad because they were rules. I talk about emergent strategy – ideas that emerge from that creative process.

Is Michael Porter's Five Forces framework still relevant today?

Porter's Five Forces is a wonderful way to analyse industries but it has nothing to do with making strategies because there's no creativity in it. It's just an input for a process, not the process itself.

You've said that you spend your public life dealing with organizations, and your private life escaping from them. Does that reflect a love–hate relationship with large organizations?

I wouldn't call it a love–hate relationship; I'd call it a hate–hate relationship. I just don't like big hierarchical organizations.

In the past, some large organizations treated people paternalistically, but reasonably decently. But many have destroyed that contract. It's significant that the two most popular management techniques of all time (Taylor's work study methods to control your hands, and strategic planning to control your brain) were adopted most enthusiastically by two groups: communist governments and American corporations.

SUMANTRA GHOSHAL: THE RISE OF THE VOLUNTEER INVESTOR

The Indian business academic, Sumantra Ghoshal, is among a handful of world-class thought-leaders based at European business schools. In 2001, Ghoshal was ranked twelfth in the Thinkers 50, the first global ranking of business thinkers.

Ghoshal holds the Robert P. Bauman Chair in Strategic Leadership at the London Business School, where he is a member of the Strategy and International Management faculty, having previously taught at INSEAD and MIT's Sloan School of Management. He is also the founding dean of the Indian School of Business in Hyderabad.

Described by The Economist as a 'Euro guru', Ghoshal is best known for his work with Christopher Bartlett of Harvard Business School. Their 1988 book, Managing Across Borders: The Transnational Solution, was named by the Financial Times as one of the 50 most influential business books of the century. Their 1997 book, The Individualized Corporation (1997), which confirmed their place among the world's most influential business thinkers, predicted the rise of a new organizational model based around purpose, people and process.

More recently, Professor Ghoshal has focused on the people part of the business equation. He has collaborated with Professor Heike Bruch of the University of St Gallen, Switzerland, to examine how the most effective managers create organizational energy through 'purposeful action'. Their forthcoming book, Bias for Action, will be published in 2004.

Your work anticipates far-reaching changes in the way that companies organize themselves and their resources. Does this change the way we understand management itself?

The dominant philosophy that has driven businesses for the past 50 years is based on the notion that a company is purely an economic entity. At its heart is the notion that ultimately, the job of management is to leverage the scarce resource and that the scarce resource is capital. We have created a whole doctrine of management based around that principle.

That premise has led to a corporate philosophy based around strategy, structure and systems. The job of leadership is to get the strategy right, and to design the right structure – and to tie the strategy with the structure through highly defined systems to deliver performance. That philosophy came basically from Alfred Sloan and his experiments at General Motors. But that philosophy is no longer appropriate today.

What has changed?

Financial capital is no longer the scarce resource. We have seen that in recent years. We have seen billions of dollars chasing what is really the scarce resource today, and will be even more so in the next 50 years, which is ideas, knowledge, entrepreneurship, and human capital.

This shift from financial capital to human capital as the scarce resource has enormous implications. The core management philosophy – the strategy, systems, structure doctrine – becomes bankrupt because it is designed to maximize the returns on financial capital and manage financial capital. You can't manage talent and people – if that is the source of competitive advantage – with that philosophy.

So what will replace it?

A very different management philosophy is arising and will become dominant – what we call the purpose, process, people philosophy.

So we are moving beyond strategy to purpose; beyond structure to process; and beyond systems to people. All of which has occurred to allow the company to attract, retain and then leverage this talent. So the management philosophy will change.

Does this fundamentally change the nature of capitalism?

This will shift the basic doctrine of shareholder capitalism, and moderate it so that if people are adding the most value, then people will increasingly have to be seen as investors not as employees. Shareholders invest money and expect a return on their money and expect capital growth. People will be seen in the same way. So they will invest their human capital in the company, will expect a return on it, and expect growth of that capital.

What does that mean for shareholders?

> The notion that all the value is distributed to shareholders will have to change to accommodate this shift in source of value creation. It will be a very different model of distribution that will become dominant over the next 50 years.

That sounds good in theory. But have companies really changed the way they see their people?

> Traditionally, people have been seen as a cost. Optimization of cost is what drove how companies saw people. In some companies that's still the case. Gradually that view of people is shifting from people as costs to people as strategic resources. The company has a vision or strategy, and people are a key strategic resource, so how do we align the strategic resource to achieve our vision, to achieve our strategy? At the same time, an even more radical view of the relationship between companies and people has begun to emerge: that of people as volunteer investors. With this view, it will be the individual employee who will be at the heart of the relationship – they will have to take responsibility for the development and deployment of their human capital, and for the company's performance, and the company will have to play a supporting role.

What about us as employees – how does it change the way we view our work?

> This is accompanied by a shift with the individual employee. Each individual employee takes responsibility for his or her own life – and that's where the people as volunteer investors fit in. They choose to invest their human capital – their knowledge, their relationships, and their ability to take action. For that they expect a return, which is indeed a return in terms of sharing the value that is created through their human capital, but also to grow the human capital itself – call it the notion of employability, or whatever, but to continuously grow the human capital just like owners of financial capital have done in the past.

How will the day-to-day task of management change as a result of this shift?

> Historically there has been a cognitive bias in thinking about management, and the way it has manifested itself is that when we talked

about skills we talked about the knowledge – what do you know? People were largely seen as a seam of intellectual capital.

Increasingly, what we are beginning to see is the importance of two other elements of human capital. One is social capital – the ability of individuals to build and maintain long-term relationships with other people. Relationships based on trust and reciprocity. We've always known that relationships are important in business, but somehow we have not counted it explicitly. Increasingly, what we are seeing from research is that one of the best indicators of superior performance beyond knowledge is this ability to build and manage relationships. That will become a focal point and people will understand it as a strategic resource, and companies will understand it and try to develop it.

And the other element of human capital?

The other area is action-taking ability. Companies still complain that although the vast majority of managers roughly know what they need to do, the trouble is that knowing what to do is one thing but most don't do it. So the ability to take action is another skill that is coming to the fore: the capacity to take action, the capacity to build personal energy for taking action, the capacity to develop and maintain focus in the midst of distracting events of managerial life. Action-taking ability – call it emotional capital if you wish.

So to sum up, historically we have seen intellectual capital as the key resource as it is, but we will increasingly recognize the importance of both social and emotional capital – the development and management of relationships and action-taking ability – as the new important elements of competence that managers will need.

What challenges does that present for companies?

The moment you recognize that the value-creating resource is people, it affects everything from how to attract whatever is the best talent in our context. Talent is not always and necessarily the graduates of the Harvard Business School or the elite institutions. So how do we identify and attract the top talent? And how do we then convert individual intellects into collective intellects. How do we link talent so that skills and knowledge of different people can be combined to create new knowledge? And then how do we bond them into the company?

How do we create an alignment between those people and their individual aspirations as volunteer investors and the overall goals and purpose of the company? Accumulating talent, orienting talent, bonding talent – that goes right across in terms of recruitment, training and development, career path management, mentoring right across the spectrum of people management processes. That will require very different approaches which will emerge as purpose, people, processes come to the fore.

Does this in turn change the relationship between business and society?

Very much. Two things are coming together. People are recognizing that to achieve superior performance, the social fabric of the organization is absolutely vital. Even to the economic goals. To maximize wealth creation by the company, at its heart in the knowledge-based service-intensive industry is the quality of the social fabric. The quality of the social fabric, the individuals, their roles and the relationships that connect them. So that's one side.

The other side is a growing awareness that companies are the most important institutions of modern society. Much of the wealth of societies is created and distributed by companies. Companies play an extremely important role in the modern economy. With that recognition, gradually the amoral notion of management – businesses only as businesses – will give way to the notion of the need to align the purpose of companies with the broader aspirations of those with which it is partnering. So both from outside and from within, the nature of the social fabric will become increasingly vital and is already becoming so.

What about at the more philosophical level? It seems that the real debate about globalization is only just beginning?

At the philosophical level it has to be understood that business has to have a role that is beyond what is just the most useful for me – whether it's short-term profits or even long-term shareholder value. They have to understand that historically whenever the most important institution of the time has not understood its role then that institution has declined. That happened with the monarchy, with organized religion, and I believe it will happen to global corporations unless leaders of global corporations recognize the profoundly important role they play in modern society and acknowledge with a show of legitimacy the social interface as an integral part of their individual and collective strategy. I believe this shift is beginning to happen.

Can globalization be a force for good?

Some people say we should all sit down together and sort it out. There is no need for throwing stones on the streets of Seattle. The trouble is we're all caught in a Catch 22. The problem for the NGOs and protestors is that the moment they are seen to work with business to solve the problems, they lose their legitimacy with their own constituency. They're caught in a Catch 22. Businesses, once they lose their rhetoric, are also caught in a Catch 22. We have to break this to begin a process.

There is still rhetoric on both sides. The rhetoric used by NGOs, economists and CEOs needs to be replaced by a recognition of the need for a partnership between them which not only benefits society but is essential for the long-term health of business. That debate has begun. I am optimistic that out of this direct confrontation, a world will arise where a business and social partnership will occur that will be economically, socially and morally better than the one we've seen for the past 50 years.

INDEX

action-taking ability 140–2
adhocracy 35–6
Alco International 74
Amazon.com 65
Ansoff, Igor 108
Apple Mac 118, 119
Arthur Andersen 73
Athos, Tony 21
attitudes 49

Bain & Co 107
Behaviourist Theory 1
Bell, Derrick 71–8
Bennis, Warren 3–6, 35, 36
Bic 116
Bin Laden, Osama 38
blogging 46
BMW 110
Bontis, Nick 85
Boston Consulting Group 107
boundary-less organizations 123–4
Boyatzis, Richard 30, 32
brain power 87–92
brands 43
    cohort 43–4
    life stage 43–4
    recognition 58
Branson, Richard 100
burn-out 83–4
Bush, George W. 6, 72
business clubs 44–5
business intelligence 33
Buzan, Tony 87–92

call centres 51
capitalism 59–62, 73
Cemex 111, 129

Champy, James 121–5
Chancey Gardner syndrome 16
change 3–6, 16, 79–82, 105
    guiding coalition 20–1
    individual initiative 19–20
    training how to think 119
    vision/creativity 19
Change Toolkit 7–8
charisma 15–16
    link with EI 25–6
chief executive officers (CEOs) 2, 11, 13, 44, 55, 62, 70, 111, 142
China 31, 39–40, 58, 86
Christensen, Clay 116
Cisco Systems 109, 124
Clinton, Bill 4, 26
communication 21, 46–7, 70
community 45, 124
    building 10
competitive advantage 81
constitutions 54–5
context 83–6
contingent thinking 39
core competencies 81
corporate
    citizenship 10
    governance 54–5
    scandals 73–5
creativity 19, 35, 117
Critchley, Bill 70
cross-engineering 123, 124–5
customers 99–100

de Geus, Arie 69
decision-making 39
Dell Computer 65, 110, 124
Dell, Michael 124

Deming, W. Edwards 111
Dick, Philip K. 38
differentiation 98–9
Drucker, Peter 35, 36, 65, 84
Druskat, Vanessa 34
Dunlap, Steve 98

e*trade 117
e-business 49
e-learning 21, 21–2
Edvinsson, Leif 83–6
efficiency programmes 109–10
elephants 53–4, 56, 57, 58
email 47, 49
emotional capital 79–82, 99, 140
emotional intelligence (EI) 2, 23–34
    development 29–30
    gender difference 25
    global aspects 30–1
    importance 32
    influences on 27–8
    link with charisma 25–6
    notion 24
    personal score 24
    in practice 33–4
    roots 25
employees 139
empowerment 10
Enron 13, 73, 102–3, 132
entrepreneurs 55–6
ethics 5–6, 41, 71–8
    ambition 71–2
    awareness 76
    greed 73
    pessimism/optimism 76–7, 78
    universal codes 72
    whistle blowing 76
executive coaching
    finding/hiring 94
    mass-produced 93–4
    origins 93
    in practice 95–6
    success 94–5, 96–7
external partner networks 10

fair outcome 130
fair process 129–31
    engagement 131
    expectation clarity 131
    principle 131
financial capital 138–42
Five Forces framework 108, 136
fleas 56–7, 58, 59–60, 62–3
Ford Motor Cars 110
fringe 42
futurists 35–6
    changing attitudes 46–51
    digital marketing 64–8
    flea/elephant culture 52–63
    fringe matters 42–5
    thinking the unthinkable 37–41

Gardner, Howard 28
Gates, Bill 59, 81
geeks and geezers 3–6
General Electric (GE) 6
General Electric (GE) Capital 93
General Motors (GM) 110, 128
genius 92
Gerstner, Lou 19, 48
Ghoshal, Sumantra 70, 137–42
Gillette 116
Giuliani, Rudy 6
globalization 41, 53–4, 67, 101, 141–2
goals 59–60
Goldsmith, Marshall 93–7
Goleman, Daniel 23–34
goodwill 130–1
Great Man theories 1
guiding coalition
    avoidance of/'snakes' 20
    power, expertise, credibility, leadership 20
    trust 20

Hamel, Gary 108, 109–13
Handy, Charles 52–63, 101
Harley-Davidson 80
Hart-Rudman Commission 38
Harvard Business School 5
Hay Group 31–2
human capital 138–42

IBM 48–9, 91, 109
ImClone 74
India 30–1, 58, 135
industry lifecycle 128
innovation 10, 35, 80–1, 110–12
    creativity 119

definition 117–18
development capability 112
radical 112–13
requisite variety 113
resource attraction 113
understanding 118–19
value 129
wealth-creation 111–12
intellectual capital 83–6, 91, 102–6
business efficiency 85
change 105
education 85
foreign trade 85
human nature 104–5
management fad 103–4
management of 106
measurement/models 105–6
R&D 85–6
Internet 48, 65, 107
anonymity 47
communication 46–7
control over 47–8
IBM involvement 48–9
reliability 48
spam 47
IQ tests 28–9

Jet Blue 110
Joy, Bill 81
Jung, C.G. 99

Kahn, Herman 36, 38
Kanter, Rosabeth Moss 7–11
Kelleher, Herb 100
Kelley, Robert 33
Kets de Vries, Manfred 12–17
Kim, W. Chan 126–31
King, Martin Luther Jr 77
Knots.com 67
knowledge management 35, 91, 103–5
knowledge tourism 86
knowledge worker 6
Kotler, Philip 64–8
Kotter, John 18–22
Kozlowski, L. Dennis 13, 74

Lawrence, Paul 21
Lay, Kenneth 13
leadership

attributes 9
definition 11
difficulties 1–2
emotional competence 23–34
expectations 8–9, 10
failures 2
heroes/villains 9–10, 12–17
individual/team 18–22
new models 2
technology takeup 7–11
theories 1
youth/age 3–7
Leiter, Richard 97
Lichenstein Global Trust 91
Long Boom 41

McBerr consultancy 31
McClelland, David 27–8, 31
Machiavellian behaviour 26
McKinsey & Company 44, 107
McLuhan, Marshall 36
management
cognitive bias 139–40
education facilities 134
in India 135
nuanced 134
self-education 134
social/economic balance 133
style 133
training 133–4
work study methods 136
Mandela, Nelson 5, 9–10
marketing 64–8
customers 66
four Ps 66
global 67
Markides, Costas 114–20
Maslow, A. 6
materialism 76
Matshushita, Konosuke 18
Mauborgne, Renée 126–31
mavericks 100
MBAs 30, 133–4
mentoring 6
mergers/acquisitions (M&As) 110
Merrill Lynch 117
Messier, Jean-Marie 13
metamarkets 67
metaphors 52–3

mechanistic 69–70
Microsoft 81
Miller Lite beer 43
mind mapping 87–8
    business aspects 90–2
    origins 88
    planning 89
    in practice 89–90, 91–2
Minority Report (film) 38
Mintzberg, Henry 108, 132–6
mobile workforce 50–1
Monte Christo Complex 14
moral corporation 119–20
museums 43

narcissism 13–17, 27
nation states 82
networks 10, 44–5, 124
new economy 135
niches 98–101
Nike 44
nine-to-five Monday-to-Friday (9–5 M-F) 51
Nokia 81, 99
Nordström, Kjell 98–101

organizational effectiveness 21

partnerships 63
Pascale, Richard 35, 69
Patrick, John 48–51
pattern analysis 18
people 69–70
    brain power 87–92
    coaching 93–7
    emotional capital 79–82
    intellectual capital 102–6
    knowledge workers 83–6
    protestors/scandals 71–8
    tribes 98–101
Peter Principle 25
Porsche 110
Porter, Michael 108, 116, 136
portfolio careers 57
Prahalad, C K 97, 108
promotion 104

quality management 111

re-engineering

downsizing 122
    effect on culture 122–3
    success/failure 121–2
recruitment 100
redundancy 56–7
relationship capital 140
Ridderstråle, Jonas 79–82
Roosevelt, Theodore 4
Ryanair 110

scenario planning 38–41
Schein, Ed 21
Schwab 117
Schwartz, Peter 37–41
self-awareness 5–6
selfishness 61–2
Semler, Ricardo 107
September 11th 4, 6, 38, 41, 47–8, 130
Shamrock organization 53
shareholder value 73–5, 132–3, 139
Shell 111
Situational Theory 1
Skilling, Jeffrey 27
Slater, Philip 35, 36
small and medium-sized enterprises (SMEs) 58
smart companies 79–82
social capital 140, 141
SouthWest Airlines 100
Spielberg, Steven 38
Stanley Works (tool makers) 73
Stewart, Martha 74
Stewart, Thomas 29, 102–6
strategic move 128–31
strategy 107–8
    balance 132–6
    differentiated 115–16
    financial/human capital shift 138–42
    growth 110–13
    jungle 114–15, 120
    military 126–7
    purposeful action/volunteer investor 137–42
    re-engineering/cross-engineering 121–5
    reinvention/innovation 109–13
    retrenchment 110–11
    rules 135
    smart moves 126–32
    system/structure relationship 137–8
    time frame 127–8
    winning 116–17

Sun 109
support systems 9–10

Taylor, Frederick W. 70, 136
team building 18–22
technology 8, 51, 101, 109
Toffler, Alvin 35, 35–6
Trait Theory 1
trends 42
tribalism 98–101
Truman, Harry 44
trust 20, 125, 140
turnarounds 8–11
Tyco 13

value-creation 140–2
vision 19–20, 44
Vivendi 13
volunteer investors 141

Wack, Pierre 39
Wacker, Watts 42–5
Wal-Mart 110
Walton, Sam 19
Whirlpool 111
Wilson, Brian 81
wireless fidelity (WiFi) 50–1
World Wide Web 7
WorldCom 74